A BRIEF HISTORY OF PACIFISM

from Jesus to Tolstoy

A BRIEF HISTORY OF PACIFISM
from Jesus to Tolstoy

by

PETER BROCK

Professor Emeritus of History

in the

University of Toronto

TORONTO
1992

Distributed by

SYRACUSE UNIVERSITY PRESS

in

North America, Asia, and the Pacific

ISBN: 0-9690997-1-1

First published in 1981 as 'THE ROOTS OF WAR RESISTANCE: PACIFISM
FROM THE EARLY CHURCH TO TOLSTOY'
Second edition August 1992

Distributors in Europe:
The Peace Pledge Union
6 Endsleigh Street
London WC1H 0DX
U.K.

CONTENTS

PREFACE

I published the first edition of this small book (under a different title) eleven years ago. It then went quickly and quietly out of print. I hope the present reprint may prove useful both to the general reader interested in learning something about the past of contemporary pacifism and to those engaged in peace studies, either as teachers or as students.

I have made a few changes for this edition but essentially the text remains the same — with the focus on what is often defined as absolute, or "integral", pacifism.

June 1992   Peter Brock

NAPOLÉON:

Ay! Not content to stand on their own strength,
They try to hire the enginry of Heaven.
I am no theologian, but I laugh
That men can be so grossly logicless,
When war, defensive or aggressive either,
Is in its essence Pagan, and opposed
To the whole gist of Christianity!

— From Thomas Hardy, *The Dynasts,*
Part Third, Act I, Scene IV

1. THE ORIGINS OF CHRISTIAN ANTIMILITARISM

An unconditional rejection of war, so far as we know, arose first among the early Christians who lived within the frontiers of the Roman Empire during the first three centuries A.D. True, the idea of peace and nonviolence can be found earlier in the history of man as well as in other cultures than the Judaeo-Christian one — for instance, among Indians and Chinese and the indigenous peoples of North America. But nowhere else do we find "pacificist" ideas leading to practical antimilitarism, to the refusal of military service as the ultimate expression of a principled repudiation of violence.

But did Jesus himself take a completely pacifist stand or intend his followers to refuse participation in war under any circumstances? This is not a simple question to answer, not merely because we know his message only at second hand through works composed by others after his death, but also because the problem of war (like slavery) is not one of his central concerns. The evidence for Jesus' pacifism, therefore, is "cumulative" (C. J. Cadoux) rather than specific. It does not depend upon any one text. It emerges from a consideration of his total outlook on God and man.

Of primary importance here is the message of nonresistance that Jesus preached. He does not mention war but it requires considerable ingenuity to show how the waging of war can be squared with his injunctions as these are presented to us in the Sermon on the Mount or the Beatitudes. "If someone slaps you on the right cheek, turn and offer him your left." "Love your enemies and pray for your persecutors." "How blest are the peacemakers; God shall call them his sons." Moreover, his attitude to the Roman army of occupation and to its Jewish collaborators indicates his rejection of violence as a political weapon. The view that Jesus was a Zealot, as the militant Jewish protonationalists of that time were known, seems most implausible. A tax-collector was among his adherents and a Roman soldier among those he cured of sickness. Loving enemies and praying for persecutors were scarcely typical of the Zealot outlook. Jesus was indeed opposed to paying Caesar what was not due to him but nonviolent suffering combined with love of the wrongdoer was his answer to the problem of political oppression and social injustice.

In his study of Luke's gospel Richard J. Cassidy points out: "In particular circumstances Jesus acts and speaks aggressively, but he always does so without doing or sanctioning violence to persons, and he continually witnesses to overriding love and forgiveness." Indeed a number of sayings scattered through the gospels, when added to key texts like the Sermon on the Mount and the Beatitudes, indicate that Jesus' teaching was one of love and nonretaliation. His death on the cross became a symbol of his rejection of violence as a means either of bringing in the Kingdom of God or of opposing alien rule. "It is clear that Jesus sharply criticized the rich and several of the political rulers of his day. It is also clear that he foresees divisions arising as a consequence of his teachings. Nevertheless, ... Jesus consistently rejects the inclinations of his followers to utilize ... violence."

Even though there are a few passages in the gospels which, if taken quite literally, are puzzling because they could seem to approve the use of the sword in self-defence, they can scarcely shake the impression of the nonviolent character of Jesus' ministry. Nonpacifist theologians in many cases admit this. Nevertheless they argue against the assumption that he intended Christians to take an unconditionally pacifist stand. These arguments may be summarized, for convenience sake, under four headings (with the understanding that they are not shared *in toto* by every nonpacifist theologian).

9

First, there is the idea of the interim-ethic, that Jesus intended his nonviolence to be mandatory only for a short period until his second coming. However, "the way of life" he proclaims "is not at any point linked to the relativities of a temporary situation, but rooted in the very nature of God" (John Ferguson). Secondly, nonviolence has frequently been regarded as a counsel of perfection. The Roman Catholic Church, for instance, has always recognized the validity of vocational pacifism — but only in the case of its monastic orders. Yet a qualification of this kind does not appear in Jesus' own words. "You must therefore be all goodness," he says, "just as your heavenly Father is all good." Again, some have seen Christian nonresistance as a purely personal ethic applicable only in relations between individuals. This was Luther's stand: it has been Reinhold Niebuhr's, too, after his abandonment of pacifism. According to this view, a Christian may fight at the command of a government while obligated to turn the other cheek if personally attacked. Such a distinction, however, appears to be absent from the New Testament record. Finally comes the frequently held opinion that loving and killing are not mutually exclusive activities. In a just cause — or, it has been sometimes urged, for the faith — the Christian may wield the sword in a loving spirit. On the other hand, that war leads inevitably to a denial of love became, we shall see, one of the strongest arguments in the armoury of Christian pacifism.

The composition of the New Testament, we should note, dates towards the end of the first century A.D. Parts of it may even have been written in the early years of the second century. If a pacifist interpretation of Jesus' ministry as presented in the gospels is correct — as has been argued above — then the pacifist stance of the church during the first century and more after Jesus' death is incontrovertible. For the pages of the New Testament reflect the ethos of the Christian church of that time as much as, perhaps even more than, they reflect Jesus' own teachings. This consideration is important, for we do not hear of Christians actually objecting to military service until after 170 during the last years of the reign of the philosopher-emperor Marcus Aurelius. (We should add, though, available evidence indicates that Christian Jews took a noncombatant position during the protonationalist revolt of 66-70 that was ruthlessly crushed by the Romans.) Before Marcus Aurelius' reign it seems that military service did not present a serious problem for Christians. At first membership of the church was drawn from sections of the population which remained outside the political life of the Empire — Jews, slaves, and the poorest sections of the community as well as women. If anyone in office was baptized he withdrew from official life. Thus for some time the church was not compelled to deal directly with the question whether its members could carry out the duties of a magistrate or serve the state with arms.

The era of the early church, that is, from Jesus' execution in 29 to Emperor Constantine the Great's granting of official status to the Christian religion in 313, covered almost as long a stretch of time as has elapsed today since the founding of Quaker Pennsylvania. A thematic approach with respect to so long a period obviously has its dangers, for it may obliterate the transformations which ideas and institutions undergo in the course of time. But this, rather than a chronological treatment, would seem to be more effective for our discussion of the antimilitarist ideology of the early Christian church.

At first, as we might expect, the early church fathers did not broach pacifism directly. But from the beginning they do extol the virtues of peace and condemn the iniquities of war. In the first decade of the second century Ignatius declared: "Nothing is better than peace, by which all war . . . is abolished." He was writing at the period when the books of the New Testament were being completed. Thus the witness for peace is unbroken. Some three decades later we find Justin Martyr speaking out even more forthrightly concerning his fellow believers: "We who used to kill one another do not make war on our enemies." Christians had turned their swords into ploughshares and abandoned the ways of war.

On this subject there is virtual unanimity among the church's spokesmen. (The only exception, Julianus Africanus, is a quite unrepresentative figure.) Killing in battle is equated with murder and soldiering is regarded as the work of the devil. Among their reasons for condemning the imperial administration is the fact that it wages war against its enemies instead of becoming reconciled to them as a Christian should do. They hold up universal peace as the aim of earthly endeavour. However, since the distinction between soldier and policeman did not exist in those days — soldiers also fulfilled the functions of maintaining law and order within the state's boundaries — some ambiguity existed on this point in the minds of early Christian writers. Soldiers appeared to have legitimate duties as well as those which might rightly incur the censure of the church.

Evidently the idea of pacifism forming part of an interim-ethic had not occurred to such leading figures in the church as Tertullian and Origen, who lived in the first half of the third century. By the time they wrote, however, the "soldier-question" had already emerged as a problem for the church. For, at the very same time as we first hear of Christians objecting to military service, that is in the last decade of Marcus Aurelius' reign, we learn, too, that there were also Christians serving in the imperial armies. It is improbable that persons who were already members of the church consented to join the forces, but it seems that the church was prepared to receive into at least associate membership serving soldiers who accepted the faith, and that it did not require them to leave the army. This is how some scholars at any rate have interpreted church rules of the period, which are not entirely clear, however, since they have survived only in a later version. The fact that during the long years of peace Roman soldiers would be engaged mainly in police duties and might never have to shed the blood of a foreign foe, made such a compromise easier for the church: their profession would not require them to break the commandment not to kill.

There were obviously perils, however, in a permissive position of this kind. Tertullian, who did not at first come down explicitly against military service (he merely notes the existence of Christians in the army), "later, when he recognized its dangers and its fundamental incompatibility, in his mind, with loyalty to Christ, firmly and totally came to oppose it" (Stephen Gero). In his famous treatise *Concerning Idolatry,* which he composed around the turn of the second century A.D., he condemned even peacetime soldiering. "Christ in disarming Peter ungirt every soldier." If an army convert to Christianity was not permitted to resign, he must willingly suffer the consequences of disobeying orders which might involve martyrdom in the end.

This rigorism is echoed and amplified half a century later by Origen in a work entitled *Against Celsus.* Celsus was a pagan philosopher who, writing around the year 178, had blamed Christians for undermining the security of the Empire by refusing to defend it by arms. (Incidentally, it is this attack of his which provides the first definitive evidence of Christian conscientious objection.) Origen takes up Celsus' charge and turns it against him. By their prayers to the true God and their upright way of life Christians, he writes, were contributing more to the defense of the Empire against barbarian invaders than all its ruler's soldiers. The only reliable defense was trust in the power of God.

Even as late as the second half of the third century the church remained staunchly antimilitarist. "Respect for life" was still at the centre of its message

(Jean-Michel Hornus). Only very uneasily did the church at this time accommodate itself to the existence of Christian sympathizers in the army or in public offices entailing the use of force. Yet there were elements in its doctrine which were eventually to make the transition from antimilitarism to recognition of the Christian militant easier than this might otherwise have been.

In the first place, even uncompromisingly pacifist writers like Origen concede that the state and military forces were justified on a lower plane of morality than the Christian one. What might happen, then, if the Emperor converted to Christianity? Again, the antimilitarist church fathers unanimously approved a number of the wars waged by the Jews in Old Testament times. Of course, they pointed out that Christ had brought a new dispensation that excluded the use of force along with other social institutions like concubinage or polygamy which the Old Testament allowed. Still, the distinction between God's approval of war B.C. and his disapproval A.D. might sometimes become blurred. In addition, we find abundant use being made by these writers of military metaphors. They illustrate their points by introducing military phraseology. Christians, for instance, are frequently described as "soldiers of Christ". If we consider, too, that they drew on the Bible's apocalyptic books — the book of Revelation is the best example of this kind of literature — and that some of them, as a result of this reading, foresaw a terrestial return of Christ in glory and the consequent extirpation of his enemies, we shall understand it was not so difficult to give all this a twist justifying Christian militancy. Of course Tertullian and Origen and the others, as it were, spiritualized these apocalyptic conflicts and did not envisage the use of real weapons in waging them. Yet "this belief in a warrior-Christ, who would conquer his enemies played a certain part in preventing a unanimous and uncompromising rejection of warfare as a permissible element in Christian life" (Cadoux).

It has sometimes been argued that the main consideration leading early Christians to refuse military service was their fear of idolatry: "in no case is there recorded any soldier's refusing to kill" (John Helgeland). Roman officers were indeed required to make sacrificial offerings, and these were objectionable to the church on account of their association with paganism. Yet for a long period the requirement had lapsed: it again became a problem for Christians in the army only towards the end of the third and at the beginning of the fourth century when it was enforced fairly regularly. The evidence for the most part indicates that the early Christian conscientious objectors refused service because soldiering involved the taking of human life and an infringement of Jesus' injunction to love enemies. For instance, the twenty-one year old North African, Maximilianus, later canonized by the church, on being called up for military service in 295 refused, saying: "I cannot serve. I cannot commit a sin. I am a Christian." This led to his execution. In the account of his martyrdom we do not hear of any objection to pagan sacrifice as grounds for his refusing to become a soldier. As Paolo Siniscalco has noted, Maximilianus' refusal of military service was rooted in "a vision of the world which has in God its sole point of reference."

The period of early Christian antimilitarism ends in 313. In that year the sunworshipper, Emperor Constantine, became patron of the church — after winning victory over his rivals to the throne as a result of what he liked to consider the intervention of the Christians' God. Constantine himself did not accept baptism until the very end of his life and Christianity did not become the exclusive religion of the Empire until long afterwards. But henceforward (with the exception of the brief reign of Julian the Apostate) Christianity was in a privileged position in the state. Under Constantine the soldiers of Christ, as Adolf Harnack has remarked, "placed themselves at the service of the emperor."

12

The new situation did not mean the immediate disappearance of Christian pacifism. Even the tutor to Constantine's son, the eminent theologian Lactantius, defended the conscientious objector and condemned the death penalty as unchristian. "God prohibits killing", he wrote. "And so it will not be lawful for a just man to serve as a soldier — for justice itself is his military service — nor to accuse anyone of a capital offence, because it makes no difference whether you kill with a sword or with a word." Throughout the fourth century and into the fifth we occasionally find instances of young Christian men taking the conscientious-objector stand. But they now represent a minority position, whereas earlier those taking this stand could expect the full backing of the church authorities. The latter supported war now. From 438 on, the imperial army came to be recruited exclusively from Christians. Already St. Augustine of Hippo, a North African like the canonized conscientious objector Maximilianus, had begun to enunciate the doctrine of the "just war" which, further elaborated in the ensuing centuries, has remained down to the present the officially recognized teaching of the Roman Catholic church on the subject of international conflict.

Christianity could scarcely have become the state religion of a realm like the Roman Empire without shedding its pacifist beliefs. Recognition of the kind granted by Constantine the Great and his successors brought the church security against renewed persecution and the possibility of greatly extending its influence. Yet this was bought at a price. For the pacifist rigorists it meant "the fall of Christianity."

The barbarian invasions occasioned the downfall of the Western Roman Empire."The barbarians militarized Christianity" (Roland H. Bainton); as a result, Christian pacifism was submerged for nearly a millennium. When it emerged again it was among the sects which proliferated in late medieval Europe. The Catholic church, it is true, permitted a vocational noncombatancy for monks and friars; in fact, its clergy in general were exempt from participating in battle. But the radical antimilitarism of the early church found no place in its teachings.

The pacifist idea was reintroduced by the Waldenses, a sect which rose in southern France towards the end of the twelfth century. Their founder was a well-to-do merchant of Lyon, Pierre Waldes. His followers were mostly simple men, often ill educated, who took the New Testament literally, including its injunction not to resist evil. Perhaps there was an influence here of an older sect, the Cathars, some of whose members refused to take human life — mainly, it would seem, on account of their objection to spilling blood. The Cathars derived from the East and professed a faith that was not properly speaking Christian for it originated from the dualistic teaching of the third-century (A.D.) Mesopotamian prophet, Mani. The Waldenses' beliefs, on the other hand, were strictly Bible-centered, and they strove to pattern their lives on the model they found in the New Testament. The sect spread first to northern Italy where it found a ready reception among the artisans of Lombardy and then to central Europe where it gained adherents chiefly among the German-speaking peasantry. It was fiercely persecuted by the ecclesiastical authorities who succeeded in destroying nearly all the religious literature it produced for the edification of its members. We are thus almost entirely dependent for a knowledge of its doctrines on the evidence provided by its enemies, the church inquisitors. From their records we learn, however, that the Waldenses refused under any pretext to take human life. "No man ought to be killed, not excluding malefactors", one of them said. The sect condemned the secular authorities for executing criminals as well as for waging war. It blamed the early church for eventually accepting the tutelage of the state and for not continuing to accept the consequences of a strict adherence to gospel principles.

The Waldenses towards the end of the fifteenth century abandoned their pacifism and attempted to ward off mounting persecution by violent resistance to their oppressors. In this they were only partly successful since the sect was effectively suppressed except for a few surviving communities situated in the Alps.

Before then a new focus of Christian pacifism had arisen in the kingdom of Bohemia, which then formed an independent unit within the Holy Roman Empire. The Czechs, who formed the majority of Bohemia's inhabitants, had broken with Rome following the execution as a heretic of the leader of their religious reform movement, John Hus. (His death by burning took place in 1415 in the course of the church council held at Constance.) Bohemia also contained a sizeable German minority, especially in the frontier districts. Along the kingdom's southern borders Waldensian communities of German origin had existed since the thirteenth century. These may very likely have contributed to the emergence of pacifism in Bohemia, though scholars disagree how far the German sectaries succeeded in converting their Czech speaking peasant neighbours to their faith. But it seems unlikely it is a mere coincidence that it was from the same area where the Waldenses were settled that the radical branch of Hussitism originated.

Hus himself did not take a pacifist position. But the south Bohemian radicals, who became known as Taborites from the town they founded of this name, for a brief while preached "Thou shalt not kill." They also urged the equality of all believers along with community of goods. This was during the years 1418 and 1419 when masses of discontented peasants abandoned their farms in expectation of Christ's imminent return to earth in order to establish a terrestial Kingdom of God. But early in 1420 their situation changed: a threatening army of foreign crusaders had invaded the land determined to overthrow the followers of Hus, whether moderates or radicals, and to reinstate the orthodox Catholic faith. Not only did the radicals modify to some extent their social egalitarianism in order to maintain the support of sympathetic nobles (one of these, the famous John Žižka, became their military commander). They also began to arm, together with the nonpacifist moderates, in order to repel the invaders. A leading Taborite priest now told the brethren: "It is time to lay aside pilgrims' staffs and to take up arms, for the enemy grows in numbers and goats are bearing down on the flourishing vineyard of the Lord."

Hussite militancy was universal at this point. We know of only one dissentient. His name was Peter Chelčický. Possibly even Chelčický had wavered for a short time, but, if so, he soon regained his faith in nonviolence. (After becoming acquainted with Chelčický's writings Tolstoy spoke warmly of their depth of content and their "wonderful force and beauty.") Unfortunately we know very little about Chelčický's life. Indeed even his exact identity is uncertain. He may have been a farmer but more probably he sprang from a family of knights who held landed property in south Bohemia, not too far from Tabor. If the latter supposition is right, he must have renounced the privileges of his class and voluntarily adopted the simple life. His radical viewpoint resulted from his reading of the gospels — and from his contacts with the Taborite movement in its earliest, restorationist phase. What Chelčický preached throughout his life was just the restoration of the primitive Christian community as it is depicted in the pages of the New Testament, including the renunciation of the sword even to bring in the Kingdom of God or in defence against foreign invasion. It was on this issue that in 1420 Chelčický, then in his thirties, had clashed with the leading theologian of the Hussite camp, Jacobellus. Though a moderate in politics and theology, Jacobellus agreed with the radicals in their trust in the sword.

14

Over the next three decades Chelčický produced a number of works in which he expounded his view of Christianity. His masterpiece, a lengthy treatise he entitled *The Net of Faith* (the net which was broken by the false followers of Christ who did not keep his commandments), dates from the early 1440's. In all his writings the same ideas recur: this perhaps makes them somewhat tedious for the modern reader. Chelčický calls for a return to primitive Christianity. The religion preached by Jesus, he says, was one of love and forgiveness of enemies. For his followers the "Law of Love" had replaced the Old Testament dispensation which allowed revenge on evildoers. Therefore, not only must Christians, to be worthy of the name, apply this law to their personal conduct. It should regulate the social institutions of Christendom, too. Judged by this standard the state itself stood condemned. It was pagan and permissible only for those who did not claim to be Christians. "The temporal order of force and Christ's way of love are far removed from each other." Chelčický was remorseless in his critique of the feudal social system which still prevailed in fifteenth-century Europe as well as of the economic exploitation of the peasantry on which this system was based. "The fullness of authority", he wrote, "lies in the accumulation of wealth and vast gatherings of armed men, castles, and walled towns, while the fullness and completion of faith lies in God's wisdom and the strength of the Holy Spirit." He praised the life of the ordinary villager and castigated the vices of the affluent and the pride of men of learning and culture. He suspected town life for the temptations which it presented to the unwary. He himself founded a community in the countryside where he and his followers could practice simple living.

Endemic warfare ravaged Bohemia throughout this period. For Chelčický war appeared as the mark of the Beast, the Antichrist who had taken possession of those "benighted Christians" unwilling to follow in the footsteps of their master. If St. Peter himself, wrote Chelčický, "should suddenly appear from Heaven and begin to advocate the sword and to gather together an army in order to defend the truth and establish God's order by worldly might, even then I would not believe him." Love and nonviolence were for him the only answer to evil. He especially condemned the state's conscription of artisans and peasants for service in its wars. It did not matter to him that the Bohemian state was a Hussite one. For all his admiration for Hus he openly expressed his disagreement with the martyred leader for his failure to accept the nonresistant position.

Perhaps it is anachronistic to call Chelčický an anarchist on account of his rejection of the state, since his ethos was predominantly otherworldly. Yet he foreshadows the anarchist current in modern political thought. And his gospel-centred nonresistance is certainly a landmark in the evolution of pacifist thought.[*]

Chelčický's spiritual and intellectual heritage was carried on in Bohemia. His heir was a sect known as the Unity of Czech Brethren. The Unity, whose members remained almost exclusively Czech until its suppression in the 1620's by the victorious Counter-Reformation, came into existence between 1457 and 1467. Chelčický died during these years (the exact date of his death is unknown) and his followers, along with other religious seekers who were to find a spiritual home there, merged with the new religious organization. The Unity's founder was Brother Gregory, an excellent organizer and a man able to transmit to others his enthusiasm for the cause. The time indeed proved opportune. The Taborite movement had finally disintegrated around the middle of the century: some of its sup-

---

[*]There is so far no English translation of the *Net of Faith*. But see the German rendering by Carl Vogl: *Das Netz des Glaubens* (Dachau, 1924; reprint, Hildersheim and New York, 1970).

porters, disillusioned by now with leftwing violence, gravitated towards the Unity. Moreover, the head of the official Hussite church was at first quite sympathetic (in fact Brother Gregory was his nephew) and the ruler, the Hussite King George, showed tolerance in religious matters unusual in that age. True, the Unity in its early years did suffer sporadic persecution but this proved insufficient for eradicating the new movement. In addition, the end of the Bohemian wars of religion left the two parties, Hussite and Catholic, nicely balanced — with *de facto* religious toleration emerging as a result.

Brother Gregory, however, was not an original thinker. He took over Chelčický's ideas on a Christian society almost without change. The Czech Brethren, therefore, regarded the state, as Chelčický had done, as an unchristian institution and renounced war as an unchristian occupation. Since the Unity was recruited at first mainly from the lower ranks of society — artisans and peasants and poor students — they did not have to trouble much about the problems of office holding. Briefly, at the end of the 1460's when the country — for the last time — was faced with a crusading army bent on extirpating Hussitism, some members probably had to face conscription for the militia. But the ensuing decades were peaceful and the issue did not arise again. The Brethren of that time lived apart from society, spiritually if not physically. They could leave fighting and governing to their social superiors. Their task was to follow "the narrow path" pointed out by Chelčický.

Yet under the surface the composition of the Unity was changing during the 1470's and 1480's. It was no longer exclusively a fellowship of honest ploughmen and unlettered artisans whose leaders were simple men, like Brother Gregory, well read in the Scriptures but eschewing other, more worldly forms of learning. Gregory before he died in 1474, we might almost think, had been too successful in his work of organizing and recruiting, had cast his net too widely so that some of those caught, unable to bear the sect's moral rigorism, might strain to break it.

In fact we find three elements, whose outlook was not entirely in consonance with the outlook of the Unity's founding fathers, slowly increasing their influence within it. In the first place the number of Brethren living in towns grew. This is indicated by the records, even though of course no figures of membership exist. However modest, the needs of urban Brethren were more extensive, their horizens wider, than those of the country members. Moreover, in towns the citizens were sometimes required to serve in the administration or to help in defense. But office holding was forbidden the Brethren along with mustering in the town militia, for both could lead to bloodshed. Secondly, the number of educated members, though still very small in proportion to the total, rose. Men who had taken degrees at the university and come into contact with the new humanist learning beginning to penetrate central Europe were unlikely to be very sympathetic to the old Brethren contempt for upper class culture. There were exceptions naturally. But young university graduates like Brother Luke who came to the fore at the beginning of the 1490's chafed increasingly at what they considered the limited outlook of their church, at its antiintellectualism. Still intensely devout, they sought to bring the Unity into the mainstream of the Czech religious culture of their day. They did not sympathize with Chelčický's antistate ideology which they felt impeded the outreach of the Unity in the name of an outmoded literalism. They aspired to gain the allegiance of a section of society hitherto almost unrepresented among the brethren — the nobility. And this seemed impossible so long as the landed nobility was required by the Unity not only to lay aside the sword but to give up its estates when ownership entailed exercise of the magistrate's office, as it almost always did in those days. Relaxation of the church's sociopolitical discipline, then, would enable pious noblemen and noblewomen to apply for membership; and their presence within the Unity would guarantee its protection in a country like Bohemia where the nobility had almost wholly taken over the government of the country.

The storm burst in 1490. In that year one of the Unity's main urban congregations appealed to the church leaders for advice how its members should respond to demands from the municipality to take part in local administration. They had refused hitherto but the situation was becoming more tense. The leadership of the Unity was divided in opinion. The older generation led by Bishop Matthias was against participation unless there was absolutely no other way out. The younger leaders thought differently. As one of them put it: "If we forbid the brethren to take part in the administration of justice, we shall be placing an unbearable yoke upon their necks." An evasive answer to the appeal was given at first, obviously in an attempt to reach a compromise between the divergent views represented on the church's ruling council. But the "modernizers" — Brother Luke and his friends — won the day in the end. True, permission to participate in city government, when it came, was hedged around with qualifications. But the old Brethren, the supporters of rigorism, who upheld Chelčický's position, were right in suspecting that this represented the thin edge of the wedge. Eventually the qualifications disappeared. And meanwhile their opponents began to extend the dispute to other questions: war and capital punishment, for instance, as well as oaths. (Chelčický and the early Brethren followed Jesus' words: "Swear not at all.")

Two parties formed: one was led by Brother Luke and the other by Brother Amos, a country member whose strength lay mainly in the village congregations, with the vacillating Bishop Matthias in the end going over to Luke's side. Even in the countryside the rigorists eventually proved to be in the minority. At the beginning the struggle for leadership had swung from one party to the other. But by mid-decade the matter had been settled in favour of Luke, and by 1500 the Amosites had left the main body of the Unity. They lingered on as a small sect for another four or five decades by which time Amos himself had long been in the grave.

The modernizers carried out their revision of the Unity's sociopolitical doctrine under the slogan of mutual toleration. Let the rigorists respect their viewpoint, they said, and they in turn would allow freedom to any who wished to pursue a "higher righteousness" than was attainable by ordinary Christians. But henceforward, to quote Brother Luke's words, "the civil power with its laws and punishments can be allowed in our Unity . . . A lord owning estates, castles, fortresses, and towns may be accepted into our Unity without having to relinquish the sword, and may become a Brother while he continues to order punishments and executions." Military service was now permissible if a church member were conscripted and were then unable to hire a substitute. And war, though the outcome of man's sin, was henceforward regarded as an unavoidable evil. Conscripts, "who being under compulsion cannot escape, yet have no thought of murder . . . nor of any unrighteousness", were no longer considered as infringing the regulations of the Unity.

The country Brethren who remained loyal to the old sociopolitical ideology lacked Luke's dynamism and his ability to communicate ideas. They also lacked the flexibility to redefine their ideology under changed circumstances, in this case the expansion of the Unity and acceptance of its faith by sections of the community lightly, if at all, represented at an earlier period. Separation from the world such as Amos and his associates called for did not prove an adequate response in the conditions of the 1490's: it did not make sense either to the church's young intellectual leadership or to Brethren in the towns who faced issues more complex than the rural Brethren had done. As a result the modernizers discarded opposition to war along with less essential tenets of the old Brethren faith.

The change in social ethos came gradually: the transformation was not completed until the second quarter of the sixteenth century. Moreover, whereas pacifism and rejection of the state were abandoned, the Unity retained a strict moral discipline until its suppression in the 1620's. Even nobles were subject to this. In the sixteenth and early seventeenth centuries the Unity, now freed from the anti-intellectualism it had inherited from Chelčický, made an important contribution to the development of Czech literature and music. The hymn writer Jan Blahoslav in the sixteenth, and the world famous educationalist Comenius in the seventeenth century, were both bishops of the Unity. Culturally the work of the sect's modernizers signified an advance. But something was lost: the simplicity and innocence of its beginnings. While the Unity's spiritual affairs were now guided by a well educated clergy, many of them humanists of high calibre, the laity who gave it direction were drawn from "prosperous capitalists, . . . decorous burgomasters, and . . . capable generals and statesmen" (Anton Gindely). The Unity had become socially respectable, the church of a moral and cultural elite. Yet its social respectability did not save it from extinction after the Bohemian Protestants were defeated at the Battle of the White Mountain in 1620, a fate shared indeed by the whole Protestant camp which had defied the power of the Habsburgs and the Counter-Reformation. By this date, however, the Unity had forgotten the doctrines it had professed at the outset of its existence, at least insofar as these commanded social equality and uncompromising rejection of war.

2. ANABAPTIST-MENNONITE NONRESISTANCE TO WORLD WAR I

(a) *Under the* Ancien Régime

The nonresistant doctrines of the early Anabaptists resembled closely those of the Czech Brethren. But the latter had abandoned pacifism a quarter of a century before the birth of Anabaptism. No connection in fact has ever been proved, despite attempts to do so on the part of several scholars. The genesis of Anabaptist nonresistance should be sought rather in the direct contact of its proponents with the New Testament. A reading of Erasmus and the other antiwar humanists of the early sixteenth century may have played a role as well.

Zürich in German-speaking Switzerland formed the cradle of Anabaptism. Soon after Luther had begun the Protestant Reformation in Germany, the Swiss city under the direction of its leading preacher, Zwingli, started to carry out a similar religious reform there, too. The work took roughly from 1519 to 1524.

In the eyes of some of his youthful followers, however, Zwingli did not go far enough. Led by a cultured young patrician, Conrad Grebel, they demanded a full restitution of the life of the apostolic church. At first perhaps they still hoped this could be accomplished through the efforts of the town council but they soon realized that neither the city fathers nor Zwingli himself were ready to sponsor a radical church policy of this kind. Grebel and his friends, therefore, broke with the leader they had hitherto revered and at the beginning of 1525 took a truly revolutionary step by baptising all who accepted their fellowship. Theirs was to be a church of adult believers, independent of the state: this rejection of infant baptism, practiced hitherto by all Christians, gave them their name, Anabaptists or rebaptizers.

From the beginning they were peaceful revolutionaries — unlike some contemporary religious radicals. From the beginning, too, Grebel regarded nonresistance as part of Jesus' teaching and the practice of the primitive Christians: it formed, therefore, an essential element of his restitutionist doctrine. A few months before his break with Zwingli he wrote: "The gospel and its adherents are not to be protected by the sword, nor are they thus to protect themselves . . . True Christian teachers are sheep among wolves, sheep for the slaughter . . . They do not use worldly sword or war, since all killing has ceased with them."

Complete unanimity as to their "doctrine of the sword" was not reached at once among these Swiss Brethren (as they liked to call themselves). At first a few Brethren dissented from Grebel's unconditional rejection of violence. Virtual consensus on this issue was reached, however, in 1527 when the Brethren, meeting at Schleitheim in February of that year, issued a confession of faith which contained an unambiguous statement of their belief that nonresistance was mandatory for all who strove to follow Jesus' example exactly. For such the magistrate's sword, whether used against an external enemy or for the preservation of internal order, was prohibited. Within the community of true Christians the only weapon against an evildoer was first the warning and then "excommunication of the one who has sinned." However, it was agreed, "the sword is ordained of God outside the perfection of Christ. It punishes and puts to death the wicked, and guards and protects the good." Therefore, the magistrate's sword was conditionally approved; only, the Brethren could have no part in its use. Theirs was a higher righteousness than that of the heathen or of merely nominal Christians, under which heading of course they included all who did not belong to their community.

Nonresistance formed part of a broader *Weltanschauung,* and it can only be understood in the context of the Brethren's whole philosophy of life, of what has been well called the Anabaptist vision. The Swiss Brethren and those who followed in their tradition strove to recreate exactly the New Testament model of living. All social institutions were to be judged by a single criterion: were they in consonance with what the gospels demanded? For the Brethren the Sermon on the Mount constituted the core of Jesus' teaching: Christian discipleship, therefore, required the same willingness to exemplify love and to endure suffering without retaliation as Jesus had displayed during his life on earth. Brotherhood was the key here. The Christian community — the believer's church — formed the necessary framework. It would give the individual member strength to overcome his weakness in following the law inscribed in the pages of the gospels (for loyalty to Christ would inevitably bring persecution by the powers that be). The Anabaptist brotherhood should live apart from the world: a separation in spirit at least, if not physical as well. True Christians would remain a minority until the end of time. For the world could not be redeemed and, therefore, patient suffering must remain their fate on this earth.

Nonconformity to the world resulted from the essentially pessimistic outlook of the Anabaptist vision. The followers of Grebel turned their backs on the humanist culture which he himself had shared. Grebel died early, in 1526. The Brethren were to be drawn henceforward almost exclusively from the lower ranks of society, from artisans or peasants, for the scholar, the patrician, and the noble felt little attraction to a faith which demanded of its adherents renunciation of the world, of its culture as well as its pleasures, and offered only the prospect of martyrdom in this life in exchange for the expectation of happiness in the life to come.

The early Anabaptists suffered severe persecution. This happened mainly as a result of their separation from the state church in the territories in which they lived, a separation symbolized by the practice of adult baptism. Objection to military service, though frowned on by the authorities, was of secondary importance in this respect. We indeed find Swiss Brethren refusing to serve in the town militias as early as 1525, the year in which the sect came into being. For killing, explained one conscientious objector, was against "God's command."

Missionaries soon began to spread Anabaptist beliefs to the other Swiss cantons. They took them, too, to the south German lands as well as to Moravia where there was extensive German settlement, and then a little later to central Germany. Around the middle of the century the Inquisition uncovered Anabaptists in Italy: speedily suppressed, they remained faithful to nonresistance to the end. Throughout most of this area no barrier of language had existed to halt the spread of the new faith. Besides, the Brethren who refused to recognize the state as a Christian institution saw no reason to regard political boundaries as an impediment to proselytising. One of the most active in this work was Michael Sattler who was largely responsible for drawing up the Schleitheim Confession. Men like Sattler were convinced nonresistants, and through their influence most south German Anabaptists accepted nonviolence as an essential component of their religion. But at first at any rate a minority existed in this area who held other views, and on the frontiers of the mission field, that is, in central Germany and the Rhineland, nonresistance came more slowly. Apart from strict nonresistance on the model of the Swiss Brethren, at least three other doctrines of the sword were found at this time within the Anabaptist community.

First comes the position advocated most eloquently by the ex-professor of theology, Balthasar Hubmaier. This differed in no significant way from Luther's view: a Christian, though he should behave nonviolently in his personal relations, was obliged to use the sword for the maintenance of civil order or in defense of the state. Hubmaier, however, won little support from his fellow Anabaptists and his doctrine of the sword scarcely survived his execution as a heretic in 1528. A second, and more widespread, view was one which has been defined as "apolitical but apocalyptic" (James M. Stayer). Its proponents advocated a peaceable stance but did not reject the possibility of using violence to establish the Kingdom of God on earth. For, along with some orthodox Protestants at this time, many Anabaptists believed in the imminent return of Christ for this purpose. This kind of conditional approval of violence seems to have been shared by the fiery preacher, Hans Hut, who died in 1527, and by a still more controversial figure, Melchior Hofmann, who was responsible for carrying the Anabaptist faith to northwest Germany (from where it spread over into the Netherlands). For Hut and Hofmann nonviolence was probably only an interim-ethic. There is no evidence that they urged their followers to resort to arms but equally no clear indication they shared the nonresistant principles of the Swiss Brethren.

A third attitude towards violence was found in a few isolated Anabaptist groups in Saxony and Thuringia. Far removed from the centre of the movement they appear to have had little in common with it apart from their acceptance of adult baptism. Adherents here were drawn to some extent from the followers of the religious revolutinary, Thomas Müntzer, whose revolt had been suppressed in 1525 at the time of the Peasants' War. These people now engaged in a series of armed conspiracies which usually ended in open violence and the practice of terrorism. Although their connection with Anabaptism *sensu stricto* cannot be denied, their activities are in no way typical of the movement as a whole.

The peaceable but nonpacifist Anabaptists who followed first Hut and then Hofmann developed subsequently in one of two opposing directions. Many of them eventually became nonresistants. On the other hand, some abandoned their peaceful stance in the mid-1530's: Hofmann himself was not responsible for this development, however, since he was arrested in 1533 and kept in prison for the rest of his life. Believing the millennium to be at hand they seized control of the north German city of Münster and, under the leadership of a fanatical Dutchman, John of Leiden, attempted to establish the New Jerusalem within its walls. Before the recapture of the city by the forces of its bishop the insurgents had established a régime which included the practice of polygamy and communism.

This bizarre episode scarcely belongs to the history of pacifism. It must, however, be included in any account of Anabaptism's development. Yet the apocalyptic furor which concluded in the *débâcle* of Münster did not affect the Anabaptists of Switzerland and south Germany: their faith in nonresistance remained unshaken throughout the turmoil. This was largely due to the efforts of Pilgram Marbeck, a mining engineer from the Tirol, who led the movement in this area until his death in 1556. The Netherlands, where Hofmann's influence was strong, remained quiet, too, though many Anabaptists here sympathized with the aims at least, if not the methods, of the Münsterites. Even in the lower German Rhineland where the latter were probably in the majority, some Anabaptists continued to be peaceable.

The defeat of apocalyptic hopes, in which many had shared without necessarily approving all that was done at Münster, brought confusion and disillusionment in the ranks of the brotherhood as well as increased vigilance and persecution on the part of the authorities, whose long nurtured suspicions that Anabaptism was a subversive faith appeared to find confirmation. That Anabaptism survived the disaster can be attributed in no small degree to the activities of an ex-Catholic priest, the Frisian Menno Simons, who lived in the northern Netherlands. Eventually most branches of the movement adopted the name Mennonite: a deserved tribute to Menno's role in its renewal.

The Münsterites did not vanish at once, however, They continued to be active for several decades after the city's fall, though with decreasing intensity, finally disappearing only in the 1570's long after they had ceased to play any significant role in Anabaptism. Those who had remained peaceable in spirit as well as in deed during the period of crisis and those who subsequently became disillusioned with the way of violence now united under Menno's leadership.

Menno had denounced the violence of the Münster Anabaptists as "blasphemy" as soon as news reached him of their taking up arms. "How can Christians fight with the implements of war?" he asked. He still regarded the Münsterites as brethren but as brethren who had strayed from the way of truth. Like George Fox, the founder of Quakerism in the next century, Menno evolved gradually towards the enunciation of a fully nonviolent stance. In fact his rejection of the state as an unchristian institution was never so uncompromising as the Swiss Brethren's — or the later Mennonites'.

We may detect two stages in the development of Menno's doctrine of the sword. At first, while opposing war and soldiering as contrary to New Testament principles, he does not seem to have regarded the magistracy as wholly unchristian. Christians might in certain circumstances accept not merely a passive but an active citizenship in this world. He wrote in 1554: "We are taught and warned not to take up the literal sword, nor ever to give our consent thereto (excepting the ordinary sword of the magistrate when it must be used), but to take up . . . the sword of the Spirit, . . . namely, the Word of God." In fact, his followers were mostly drawn from the poorer sections of the community: the higher levels of the official hierarchy were accessible to few of them. Still, Menno in this period was prepared to accept members of the sword-bearing magistracy into the community of believers, if any applied for membership or were to be found already in its ranks. In this period of his life the punishment of the wicked, even by death, appeared to him another matter from killing in warfare when the innocent perished along with wrongdoers. In his last years, however, Menno's rejection of violence stiffened. Even now he did not advise a total withdrawal from all branches of government on the part of believers. But a Christian magistrate should ungird his sword and employ only means of coercion that were consistent with love and nonretaliation. To torture or hang a criminal even when he repented his crimes, as was then the practice in all so-called Christian countries, appeared "strange and unbecoming in the light of the compassionate, merciful, kind nature . . . of Christ, the meek Lamb." Punishment should be directed towards the betterment of the wrongdoer and not be inflicted for the sake of revenge. In the conditions of that age Menno's final stand precluded in effect acceptance of most government offices.

In Menno's case, therefore, we find a "developing principle of non-resistance" (Cornelius Krahn). The Mennonites after his death in 1561 completed the process and returned to the position held at the beginning of the movement's history by Grebel and his Brethren. They withdrew so far as possible from all association with the rulers of this world.

Before we continue the story of Mennonite nonresistance after the doctrine had again become the norm throughout the whole brotherhood, we must turn to consider two groups which were only loosely connected with the mainstream of the movement: the Hutterites and the much larger church of the Antitrinitarian Anabaptists who lived in the Polish-Lithuanian commonwealth.

The Hutterites had originated in Moravia in the early 1530's. The sect was then formed from Anabaptists who fled to that comparatively tolerant land — mainly from the Tirol — under the leadership of an artisan named Jacob Hutter. Driven temporarily into exile because of their firm adherence to nonviolence they adopted a communitarian way of life during their wanderings. At first this may have been done for practical reasons, but soon it became an article of their faith, indeed in their view an essential condition of Christian living. Aristocratic families, like the Kaunitzes for example, invited them to settle on their estates, despite the Hutterites' unorthodox religious views. These landowners were prepared to overlook heresy in order to keep such hardworking and God-fearing tenants on their land. Since the Hutterites lived in parts of Moravia which were overwhelmingly Czech in ethnic composition, the cultural gap between them and their neighbours engendered by their unusual religious and social practices was compounded, therefore, by the barrier of language as well. This led to a more rigid nonconformity to the world and a more exacting observance of nonresistance than was to be found among either the Swiss Brethren or the Mennonites.

The second half of the sixteenth century formed the golden age of the Hutterite Brethren. Their collectivist farm communities prospered (they were known as *Brüderhofe*); their craftsmen were famous throughout central Europe for their skill. At the same time Hutterites submitted to a stern discipline which precluded not only idleness but all forms of worldly vanity and the pride of men of learning. Their numbers now rose to between 20,000 and 30,000 members, divided among 100 communities. They attracted into fellowship not only peasants or artisans, who constituted the overwhelming majority, but some professional men and persons of culture, too. Filled with missionary zeal, their emissaries carried the Hutterite message up and down the German lands. If "the whole world were like us," their founder had said, "then would all war and injustice come to an end."

A radical peace testimony formed part of the Hutterite vision, along with their radical social practice. They went further in their pacifism than any other branch of the Anabaptist-Mennonite movement. Indeed they shunned association not merely with the world — outwardly Christian but in their view essentially pagan — but even with evangelical Anabaptists and Mennonites because these did not believe in communitarianism. They saw the communal way of life not simply as a commandment of Christ but also as an essential prerequisite for creating a warless world; private property engendered greed and greed created the strife among men whose end result was war.

In three respects the Hutterites demonstrated in practice their pacifist radicalism: they refused to pay taxes they knew were destined for war purposes, they refused to undertake labour service which would be of use to the military, and they refused to make weapons of war. In each of these cases Mennonites of the mainstream felt no pangs of conscience in fulfilling the requirements of the authorities.

"Where taxes are demanded for the special purpose of going to war, massacring and shedding blood, we give nothing", wrote Peter Riedemann, the eloquent spokesman of mid-sixteenth-century Hutteritism. "This we do neither out of malice nor obstinacy but in the fear of God, that we make not ourselves partakers of other men's sins." "Blood money" was what the Hutterites called such payments. They upheld their testimony against paying war taxes even when towards the end of the century Turkish invasion threatened the land, and they suffered meekly the requisitioning of their goods by the indignant authorities. They were equally consistent in disobeying these when they ordered them to act as drivers for vehicles requisitioned by the army or perform other duties even indirectly connected with war. However, compulsory labour of a peaceful character they carried out cheerfully. The distinction made here is illustrated even more clearly in respect to the Hutterites' attitude to armament manufature. "Since Christians must not use and practice . . . vengeance", wrote Riedemann, "they cannot make the weapons by which such vengeance and destruction may be practised by others . . . Therefore, we make neither swords, spears, muskets nor any such weapons. What, however, is made for the benefit and daily use of man, such as bread knives, axes, hoes and the like, we both can and do make . . . If they should ever be used to harm another, we do not share the harmer's guilt, so let him bear the judgment himself."

Along with all other Protestants of the Czech kingdom, the Hutterites were forced into exile in the 1620's. In 1622 they left Moravia to settle in north Hungary (present-day Slovakia), where a limited toleration continued to exist for non-Catholics. Eventually they were forced to leave Hungary, too: this happened in the 1760's during the reign of Maria Theresa who suppressed the sect on the prompting of the Jesuits. The Hutterites removed first to Wallachia and then to the Russian Empire where in 1770 they settled on the estate of a well disposed nobleman in Ukraine. In 1800 the Emperor Paul, whose mother Catherine II had invited Mennonites from Prussia to settle in her dominions on similar conditions, officially confirmed the freedom of worship and exemption from military service, which the Hutterites had already been enjoying informally. These privileges were granted provided they paid a land tax; and to this they expressed no objection. In 1802 they moved onto crown lands. Henceforward, for government purposes they were classed along with the Mennonites.

The long period of religious persecution the Hutterites were forced to endure left its mark on the community. Their intellectual horizons narrowed; their way of life became fossilized; their numbers declined. Though they did not give up their principle of nonresistance, they were driven eventually to make compromises in order to survive. We find them, for instance, in Russia prepared to pay a war tax rather than face expulsion again, provided only some face-saving formula were devised. In Russia, too, they temporarily abandoned their communitarian way of life.

In contrast to the Hutterites the Antitrinitarian Anabaptists of Poland, despite their strict moral code and their initial social radicalism, did not attempt to withdraw from the world. They remained open to the intellectual currents of the time, and these helped to shape the ideological development of their church. Antitrinitarian views were first brought to Poland in the mid-1550's by a returning scholar, Gonesius, who had become acquainted during his study years in Italy with the works of the Spaniard Servetus, the founder of Antitrinitarianism, executed in Calvin's Geneva in 1553. On his way back to his native land Gonesius visited the Hutterites in Moravia. He fell under their spell. So that he now returned to Poland not merely a convinced Antitrinitarian but an ardent disciple of Anabaptism and nonresistance as well. He ungirded his sword and wore a wooden one in its stead, and at the same time he attacked the idea of the Trinity and urged adult in place of infant baptism to his surprised listeners.

There were at that time few, if any, countries in Europe where such opinions could be voiced openly. But the Polish state, which then included Lithuania as well as most of Byelorussia and Ukraine within its frontiers, was exceptionally tolerant. Like the neighbouring kingdoms of Bohemia and Hungary, but in an even more extreme form, Poland had evolved into a gentry republic in all but name. The king was becoming increasingly a figurehead, power decentralized, and the landed nobility — especially its more wealthy members — the real rulers of the country. The peasants had been reduced to the status of serfs tied to the land they cultivated for the profit of their masters; the middle class, too, was excluded from any say in government. Social oppression, then, formed the obverse side of the picture. The nobles claimed freedom of religious opinion for themselves — there were Lutherans and Calvinists and Orthodox among them as well as adherents of the established Catholic faith — but they denied all political rights to the overwhelming majority of the population.

Thus emergent Antitrinitarianism reflects two conflicting trends: the movement of free religious thought which was made possible by the political predominance of the nobility, and the movement of protest against social injustice which was practised by this nobility against the other sections of the community. Eventually, in an attempt to preserve and develop freedom of thought the Polish Antitrinitarians sacrificed their freedom of action against the ills of society.

Anabaptist and Antitrinitarian ideas, once introduced into the country, found a number of adherents among the Calvinists, who represented the strongest Protestant denomination. True, these people formed a minority but a minority powerful enough to split the Calvinist church in two. In 1565 the Antitrinitarians broke away and formed an independent body. Though they failed to gain official recognition (both their Anabaptism and their Antitrinitarianism were detested by Protestants and Catholics alike), they survived intact for nearly a century until the rising tide of intolerance generated by the Counter-Reformation put an end to the sect in 1661.

The Polish Antitrinitarians differed from the Swiss, German or Dutch Anabaptists in their social composition. Unlike the Anabaptists, they attracted into their midst a number of noble families whose members, alongside a trained and learned clergy usually of middle class origin, provided leadership for the church. At first converts from the nobility embraced nonresistance with enthusiasm, like John Niemojewski who, freeing his serfs, then sold his lands rather than continue to bear the sin of holding fellow men as property. He was seen at the diet of 1569 "in a mean grey garment, without sword, without wallet, without attendant, rebaptized just a few days before." We read, too, of gentlemen of ancient lineage who "refused to bear arms, lest they act contrary to the Gospel and the teaching of Christ." But the Polish Brethren (as the Antitrinitarians called themselves), although they officially adopted nonresistance as part of their confession of faith, did not exclude from membership those who could not accept the full teaching. Dissentient voices were soon heard within their ranks.

The first to contest the generally accepted doctrine of the sword was Jacob Palaeologus, an erudite but somewhat cantankerous refugee from Greece. In a treatise he wrote in 1572 he even went so far as to accuse his coreligionists of treason when they refused to fight for their country preferring rather to buy their way out of service than to bear arms. He branded this stand as shameful. Such jibes coming from one who shared the church's theology were embarrassing, indeed dangerous in a country like Poland which was engaged in endemic warfare on its eastern frontiers with Muscovites, Tatars and Turks. They could lead to a general proscription of the Antitrinitarians. Therefore, defenders of nonresistance attempted a series of rebuttals in which they sought to refute Palaeologus' arguments by showing that war was essentially unchristian. Not hostility to their fatherland, therefore, but loyalty to Jesus was the motive which had led to their adopting a nonresistant stance. If Palaeologus were right, then his reproaches applied, too, to Christ — "you . . . who abandoned your own and . . . put on no armour in defense of your country, nor commanded your own to do it."

The most effective in countering Palaeologus' arguments was a learned Antitrinitarian minister, Martin Czechowic, "the most significant figure among the preachers and polemicists of the church" (Domenico Caccamo). In 1575 he published a series of *Christian Dialogues* in Polish with the purpose of instructing the church's members in the tenets of their faith. The twelfth dialogue was devoted to the subject of nonresistance and was "brilliantly written, lively, and full of temperament" (Stanisław Kot). The Christian way, urged the author, was the way of the Cross. Jesus' followers, if they were to remain faithful to their master's teachings, must renounce self-defense and refrain from any participation in state activities. Czechowic was the first pacifist writer to give detailed consideration to the question of conscientious objection. "Under the New Covenant Christ's servants are neither to fight nor to train for war", he concluded — to the alarm of those Antitrinitarians who feared statements of this kind might lead the authorities to take repressive measures against the church.

The eastern borderlands of the commonwealth, exposed to incessant attack from without and dominated politically by great marcher lords, several of whom now held Antitrinitarian views, became the centre of resistance within the church to its pacifism and social radicalism. Opposition to serfdom and war, on the other hand, was strongest in the town congregations in the west, especially in the area around Cracow, the state capital until 1596. It was the east that produced the most effective champion of social conservatism in Simon Budny, a native born Pole who enjoyed the protection of a powerful borderland baron belonging to the Antitrinitarian church named John Kiszka. In a lengthy treatise Budny entitled *Concerning the Sword-Bearing Magistracy,* which was published in 1583, he justified Christian participation in war and the magistracy. He regarded it as right, too, for members of the church to hold their fellow Christians in servile subjection according to the law of the land.

Towards the end of the century the generation of Niemojewski and other leaders who had upheld the Anabaptist position began to die off. New men came to the fore in the church, who not only regarded adult baptism as a tenet of minor importance but no longer considered nonresistance in the uncompromising fashion of the founding fathers. The threat to the very existence of Antitrinitarianism from the growing intolerance of the other churches now loomed larger, and this made reliance on the Antitrinitarian gentry, who were represented in the diet, more pressing than before and led to the subordination of the disenfranchised plebeian element *vis-à-vis* the nobly born Brethren. In any case later generations, though for the most part sincerely devoted to the church in whose principles they had been reared, lacked the zeal of the convert ready to renounce everything — wealth, status, and life itself — for the faith they had reached only after the most severe spiritual toil.

The man who became the spokesman of this ideological transformation taking place in the Antitrinitarian movement around the beginning of the seventeenth century was not a Pole but an exiled Italian, Faustus Socinus, who in 1579 had found a refuge in the hospitable commonwealth. "He knew how to unite tact and diplomacy with strictness of doctrine . . . in order to parry the accusation of subversion" (Giovanni Pioli).

26

A gentleman by birth, a scholar by avocation, possessed of a subtle and somewhat cold intellect which contrasted with the emotional fervour of the first Polish Brethren, Socinus by the application of reason to religion made his adopted church a forerunner of the eighteenth-century Enlightenment as well as of modern religious liberalism. But the Socinians, as the Polish Brethren were known throughout Western Europe after Socinus' death in 1604, while they became progressively more radical in their theological views, in their social outlook developed steadily in a conservative direction and abandoned both their protest against serfdom and their objection to war and the shedding of human blood.

Socinus, though earlier on an uncompromising pacifist, laid the foundations for these changes in a series of lectures he delivered to a selected audience shortly before his death. Without discarding nonresistance altogether — Socinus was essentially a conciliator who strove to mediate between opposing views — he so watered the doctrine down that, later, others who lacked his fine sense for ingenious distinctions were able to throw it aside without any scruples of conscience. He saw nothing wrong now in members of the church becoming magistrates if only they refrained from imposing the death penalty. He did not object to the use of torture, universally employed at that time by the judiciary, for deterring hardened criminals. He argued, too, that the carrying of weapons for self-defense to frighten robbers and other desperadoes was not unchristian, provided no serious injuries were inflicted. Indeed if the defendant maimed or even killed his assailant unintentionally, this should be regarded merely as a venial sin. Likewise the killing in self-defense of bandits or of Turks was less blameworthy than the killing of a Christian. In regard to international war Socinus avoided its unconditional justification such as Palaeologus and Budny, who had based their case largely on citations from the Old Testament, had allowed. He continued to argue from Jesus' words in favour of noncombatancy and to apply this obligation in the case of magistrates as well as private citizens. "There is no argument in the New Testament which would make us infringe this precept," he stated. Yet, once again he introduced qualifications here which virtually nullified the seemingly absolute ban on participation in war. Though in principle fighting was indeed wrong, noblemen, he argued, might still join the colours, for the disgrace they would incur by not doing so could drive them into deeds more sinful still. True, they must do their best to avoid committing homicide. But even if they were forced to kill in battle this did not constitute as deadly a sin as adultery.

In the six decades that elapsed before the expulsion of the Antitrinitarians from Poland we see little sign of pacifist activity among Socinus' followers. The Antitrinitarian gentry sought to counter the accusations made by their enemies of lack of patriotism by a display of martial courage in the many wars engaged in by Poland during this period. The spiritual leaders of the church expressed little or no protest at this even though Socinus' position remained their official doctrine. The pacifist issue was kept alive by a select few, usually Brethren of foreign origin who were less subject to the patriotic fervour now felt by the native born gentry members.

Interest in nonresistance revived again among Socinian *émigrés* who gathered in the Dutch Republic, where they continued to debate the articles of their faith whose profession was now forbidden in Poland. In exile they proceeded to spread their liberal religious opinions and influence precursors of the Enlightenment like Pierre Bayle. And here, too, they met with Dutch Mennonites as well as smaller groups like the Collegiants who held a similar testimony against war. In Amster-

27

dam the Poles published a collected edition of those writings of their church which had been composed in Latin, including within its bulky volumes the almost forgotten works of the protagonists of pacifism. These were now read avidly by the Dutch nonresistants, to whose story we must return.

In 1572, eleven years after Menno's death, the Dutch had launched their war of independence against the Spain of Philip II under the leadership of William the Silent Prince of Orange. The struggle was to be a long one: it was not until 1648 that the United Provinces — that is, the northern half of the Netherlands — finally won international recognition of its independence, though recognition had been gained *de facto* by 1609. In the second half of the seventeenth century the Dutch engaged in war first with England and then with the France of Louis XIV, a more formidable opponent since *le grand monarque* aimed at incorporating their country into his expanding empire. Thus the Mennonites in the Netherlands, unconditional nonresistants since before the outbreak of hostilities with Spain, were forced to reach some *modus vivendi* with the authorities if they wished to survive this stormy epoch. This in fact proved not too difficult in view of the conciliatory attitude displayed by William of Orange and his successors, on the one hand, and of the traditional Mennonite willingness to grant a conditional justification — "outside the perfection of Christ" — to the magistrate's office, on the other. In fact, despite occasional harassment of Mennonite conscientious objectors, chiefly by local authorities who in their patriotic zeal were sometimes inclined to overlook the letter of the law, no serious clashes took place between Mennonites and the state over the question of their refusal to bear arms.

In 1575 Prince William gave the Mennonites the right to substitute some form of civilian service for bearing arms. (This appears to be the first time any government officially recognized a right on the part of its subjects to object on grounds of conscience to military service.) Instead of having to keep watch with weapons when the citizens were called upon to do this, Mennonites were now required only to help construct ramparts and dig ditches. We do not hear at this time that they scrupled to perform such service, even though such work, while indeed noncombatant, contributed in effect to the waging of war. The Mennonite exemption applied at first only to North Holland but broadly similar arrangements were fairly soon worked out for the rest of the country: in peacetime, though, a commutation fee was more usual than noncombatant duties, and auxiliary fire service became a frequent form of wartime exemption later. Arrangements of this kind set the pattern for Mennonite conscientious objectors until the period of revolutionary wars arrived at the end of the eighteenth century.

In addition, the Dutch Mennonites displayed their devotion to their country by making free-will money offerings to the state at moments of national crisis. This happened, for instance, in 1572 at the outset of the struggle against Spain and again exactly a century later when Louis XIV invaded Holland. They did this despite the fact that they knew their money would be used for carrying on the war, just as their conscientious objectors knew the money they paid in commutation of military service would be assigned for a similar purpose. It is true that the Dutch Mennonites, for whom at the very beginning patriotism was incomprehensible in a follower of Christ, gradually shed the hostility their predecessors had felt for the state as a paganized institution and that this change in part accounts for the conciliatory attitude displayed by them from the 1570's on. But their readiness to compromise on such issues was by no means inconsistent with the essential content of the Anabaptist-Mennonite tradition of nonresistance. According to this, Caesar had the right to demand the money and property of his Christian subjects: what he did with what he took was his concern, for which he had to account only before God. The Christian nonresistant, therefore, was not answerable for the uses to which the ruler put his gifts and taxes. He was responsible, however, for his own actions. Thus, Mennonites distinguished between paying a tax in lieu of bearing arms and hiring a substitute to take their place in the ranks. The latter course they resorted to only in dire necessity — and always with a guilty conscience.

The seventeenth century brought prosperity to the Mennonite community in the Netherlands. Although the average member remained a humble artisan or husbandman, some of the brotherhood acquired wealth through commerce or industry — or even through cultivation of the family farm. The life style of Mennonite patricians, if less ostentatious, did not differ essentially from that of the non-Mennonite urban aristocracy. The church, too, now included prominent men of letters and of learning: its ministers were often persons of considerable culture. Erudition supplemented, and occasionally replaced, piety in its spiritual leadership. The brotherhood no longer formed a persecuted society, the lowly status of whose members helped it to escape complete obliteration at the hands of the state. Toleration made possible the sizeable contribution made by seventeenth- and eighteenth-century Mennonites to the intellectual development of their country. But the zeal and earnestness and the simple Bible-centred faith, which had marked earlier generations, were gradually lost. This became visible, in particular, in the theologically liberal sections of the brotherhood. For the Mennonites, always prone to fragment into small sects, had in Holland soon split into a more liberal and a more conservative branch, each divided into a number of sub-sects. The liberals were most strongly represented in the cities, the conservatives in the countryside. At first among the liberals, and eventually even among the conservatives, enthusiasm for nonresistance ebbed. It tended to become merely a custom rather than a deeply held belief. However, where its observance was still enforced by means of the church discipline and disownment was the penalty for such acts as mustering with the militia, few cared to abandon the traditional noncombtancy and risk almost certain expulsion from their church.

In the eighteenth century the liberal wing began to relax the application of the discipline. The situation varied from community to community since the Mennonites enjoyed a congregational form of church government. But where members had the right to choose between paying the commutation fine for exemption from military duties and obeying the summons to bear arms, an increasing number of liberals — though still a minority of that branch — adopted the latter course. The reason for this trend lay of course in the fact that that sense of apartness which earlier Mennonites had felt in relation to the rest of society had largely disappeared, except in some of the more remote rural congregations or in the primitivist sects which still managed to exist in the towns. There were now worldly minded members of the brotherhood — called "coarse" Mennonites in contrast to the "fine" Mennonites who clung to the traditional ways — who lived outwardly like their neighbours in regard to such matters as dress and wearing of side-arms and ways of speech, whereas formerly all Mennonites were distinguishable from the rest of society. It was from this section of the brotherhood that the first to deviate from the church's peace testimony were drawn.

Closer integration with society made the Mennonites less immune to patriotic feelings than they had been in earlier days. Even then, we have seen, they were ready to contribute financially to their country's war effort. "Where one lot of Christians, according to the dictates of their conscience, defend the fatherland with carnal weapons, while another resort to spiritual . . . prayers, there shall the dear fatherland be defended on all sides", was how the Mennonites expressed their point of view in 1710. As the eighteenth century progressed the nonpacifists of the Mennonite brotherhood were to grow more outspoken and the defenders of the traditional stance eventually fell silent.

A startling decline in numbers accompanied the developments we have just described. The brotherhood which contained around 200,000 members at the beginning of the seventeenth century had sunk to a mere 30,000 by 1820. Lack of unity, the fragmentation into as many as twenty conflicting sects, contributed to this situation. Even more important as a cause of decline was the Mennonites' waning spiritual dynamism. Not only did they cease to attract new recruits but many of their members, failing to see now any essential difference between their church and the other liberal Protestant denominations, preferred to join one of the latter since they appeared to be in a more lively spiritual condition.

The same process of adaptation to society occurred among the German Mennonites as among the Dutch, and it brought roughly similar consequences. Here, however, this took place at a rather late date. Within the boundaries of the Holy Roman Empire the sect had survived only in Protestant lands. In the Catholic states the zeal of the Counter-Reformation proved ultimately stronger than the desire of their rulers to draw financial profit from these diligent sectaries, and all who practised Anabaptism were suppressed. Only across the eastern border in the Polish commonwealth do we find Mennonites living peacefully in a Catholic kingdom. Their settlements were to be found in Danzig and along the lower reaches of the Vistula where they reclaimed the marshes and made them a scene of plenty.

Mennonite communities also lingered on in Switzerland but the egalitarian democracy of the Swiss cantons made it difficult for them to obtain exemption from service in the citizen militias. Some of these Swiss Brethren emigrated to British North America as did many of the Alsace Mennonites and Amish (a group of strict traditionalists formed at the end of the seventeenth century). Alsace had come under French control as a result of Louis XIV's annexations and the new ruler proved generally unsympathetic to the Mennonite position. The German Mennonite diaspora came eventually to include Russia where, beginning in 1788, Mennonites emigrated in search of land for their expanding population.

Unlike the Dutch Mennonites their German speaking brethren remained almost exclusively a community of peasants and craftsmen until around the end of the eighteenth century, and for longer still in Eastern Europe and North America. Indeed, beginning as early as the 1530's German "Anabaptism had changed from a movement that was largely urban into one that was largely rural" (Claus-Peter Clasen).

Their ministers were all simple people, laymen with little book learning (though, we may add, their knowledge of the Scriptures was profound). Living either in absolutist states where the prince's word was law or in an alien ethnic environment, as in Poland, Russia or North America, they did not possess the same incentive to absorb the culture of the surrounding society as their Dutch coreligionists did in democratic and at the same time tolerant Holland. Dwelling alongside neighbours who did not share their outlook on life they continued to consider themselves exiles from this world. They were able to pursue their traditional ways in comparative quiet. They were not usually required to shoulder the burdens of citizenship which were pressed on the Swiss Brethren, and they were not easily amenable, at any rate for a long time, to those imperceptible pressures exercised by a sympathetic environment, which subtly undermined the traditionalism of the Dutch Mennonites.

From the middle of the sixteenth century at least, if not earlier, the nonresistant position became the universal rule among German speaking Mennonites.

Bearing arms was forbidden as well as the holding of office, while expulsion from the fellowship of believers resulted from persistence in breaking the church's regulations in this as in other respects. "We believe", wrote the Mennonites of Emden, for instance, in their confession of faith of 1713, "that it is our duty to abstain from military service".

In most areas exemption from this duty, incumbent on other citizens of the state, was included in the charter of privilege granted the Mennonites by its prince. The charter generally allowed them *inter alia* liberty of worship — without, however, the freedom to proselytize — and the right to some noncombatant alternative to the statutory obligation to bear arms. The Dutch model of demanding some form of nonmilitary service was rarely followed. In a few cases unconditional exemption was given but this happened only, as in Russia, where the ruler was greatly in need of settlers to open up new areas hitherto uncultivated. Normally the charters followed one of three general patterns in dealing with the Mennonite conscientious objector. Sometimes the prince extended a collective guarantee of exemption in exchange for a handsome annual payment by the congregations on his demesne. The most frequent custom, however, was for the individual objector — or rather his family — to pay a fine for this privilege. A third way out, one that was disliked by the Mennonites who practised it only when presented with no alternative, was for the objector and his family to put up money to pay for a substitute to take his place in the militia or town watch, as the case might be. But we do not find they had to do this very often. Most rulers were ready to meet the Mennonites' scruples and granted them conditions they could conscientiously accept. Such arrangements after all contributed to the financial prosperity of their states. Princes extended similar privileges to other religious groups like the Jews or the Karaites (a Jewish sect) who lived in virtually autonomous communities just as the German Mennonites did. Therefore, the favourable conditions thus created for the practice of conscientious objection stemmed not from any abstract devotion to liberty on the part of these rulers but from considerations of financial profit as well as from the traditional respect shown by the *ancien régime* for inherited privilege.

(b) *In the Age of Democracy and Nationalism*

The French Revolution of 1789 introduced a new age and destroyed the intellectual foundations of the previous epoch. The democratic ideal and the spirit of nationalism were to sweep away the privileged position of social classes and religious bodies in the name of human freedom and civic equality. Throughout the European continent the nation in arms eventually took the place of mercenary armies: universal conscription became the rule everywhere. For the old fashioned creed of nonresistance as it had been handed down among the Mennonites from generation to generation this situation spelled disaster unless means were found to restate the basic principles in terms consistent with the exigencies of the new era.

A renewal of this kind did not in fact emerge, and the reason for this must be sought in the internal development of the Mennonite brotherhood from the late eighteenth century. In fact, as a result of the impact on its members of democratic and nationalist ideas belief in nonresistance withered in most sections of the brotherhood before the nation-state, increasingly militarized in the course of the nineteenth century, finally withdrew its members' right to exemption from military service. Acculturation to a nationalistic and militaristic society rather than direct pressure frm this society, though such pressure existed too, caused the decline and ultimate extinction of Mennonite nonresistance throughout the whole of Central Europe.

We shall now review the fate of the doctrine first in the Netherlands, then in southern and western Germany and in Prussia, and finally in Russia.* Nonresistance among the tiny Mennonite groups found under French, Swiss and Austrian rule did not differ essentially in its development from that of the larger communities we shall discuss in detail. But an offshoot of Mennonitism, the Nazarene sect which was centred in Hungary, has continued to maintain a steady peace testimony to the present.

In the Netherlands the process of acculturation went furthest: here rejection of nonresistance, when it came, was complete. Eventually even Menno's name was abandoned and the church became the fellowship of the *Doopsgezinden*, i.e. the Baptists. In the 1780's many urban Mennonites, including pastors and elders of the church, supported the Dutch republican cause against the House of Orange. The radical "Patriots" (as they were commonly known) were defeated, but they returned to power with the support of the French revolutionary army in 1795 when the House of Orange was expelled. Four years later the new Batavian Republic withdrew the exemption from military service the Dutch Mennonites had enjoyed since the days of William the Silent. The legislators did this with the approval of many leading members of the church who regarded the exemption as an anomaly in a democratic age and who, moreover, wished to see their co-religionists take their share in defending the nation by arms. What is surprising is the fact that although the church authorities protested at the time — somewhat lukewarmly, it must be admitted — no case of a Dutch Mennonite refusing military service has been found after 1799, despite the church's official adherence to nonresistance up to that date. True, a person if called upon for military duties still continued to have the alternative of hiring a substitute to perform them in his place. (This of course had nothing to do with a conscientious objection since according to the law anyone with sufficient funds could choose this way out.) Undoubtedly at first some Mennonite draftees hired substitutes, others went into hiding or devised means of somehow evading induction. The practice of nonresistance cannot have disappeared at once: "the real principle, however, was dead" (N. van der Zijpp).

Sympathy with nonresistance and the old ways, which had died out in the urban congregations, lingered for another half century in a few isolated rural communities. The last of these rigorists left as a group for the United States in 1854. By 1914 the Dutch Mennonites — or rather *Doopsgezinden* — had produced a number of eminent politicians, usually of a somewhat conservative hue, as well as high government officials, respected bankers and financiers, and army and navy officers. In World War I only one conscientious objector emerged from their congregations — and he was perhaps as much a Tolstoyan as a Mennonite.

Among German Mennonites the transition from nonconformity *vis-à-vis* the world to participation in the affairs of a modern society went more slowly and remained rather less thoroughgoing than in the Netherlands. The influence of Dutch Mennonites, with their liberal theology and their egalitarian outlook, on some of the German congregations, especially urban ones in the north-west, led to their abandoning the principle of nonresistance earlier and more radically than happened elsewhere. With greater prosperity and the increased educational opportunities which accompanied this, Mennonites everywhere ceased to feel the same aloofness from worldly affairs which they had experienced in earlier centuries.

---

*See Clarence Bauman, "Gewaltlosigkeit als Kennzeichen der Gemeinde", pp. 128-40 in Hans-Jürgen Goertz, ed., *Die Mennoniten* (Stuttgart, 1971).

They no longer remained immune from the currents of opinion which swept their fellow citizens. We find young Mennonites, though still only a minority, carried away by patriotic emotion first during the War of Liberation against Napoleon I and then during the long decades of underground struggle for German unification which found a climax in 1848. In that year, during discussion in the Frankfurt parliament of the new Germany's constitution, it was a Mennonite, the liberal nationalist politician Hermann von Beckerath, who proposed the nullification of his sect's traditional exemption from military duties. "It must be remembered," said von Beckerath on this occasion, "that since no universal military service existed . . . at the time when the Mennonites received the right to withdraw from military service and as a compensation had to accept certain restrictions on their citizenship rights, the Mennonite privilege did not constitute an infraction of the right of other citizens. But now that a free state is to be established whose strength rests upon equality of its citizens in rights and duties, such a special privilege becomes utterly untenable. . . . I declare that it is contrary to the welfare of the Fatherland to provide for any exemption in the fulfilment of citizenship duties, no matter on what ground."

This statement aroused little or no protest among the Mennonites outside Prussia. In the west and south of Germany the old church discipline, once enforced rigidly, which would have led to the disownment of a member who persisted in bearing arms, had broken down. Members who accepted military duties when called upon by the state now remained in good standing. After the attempt of the men of '48 to create a united Germany had collapsed, the Mennonites' old privileged position *vis-à-vis* military service survived here for another two decades. But the number of young men who took advantage of it declined steadily. With respect to southern Germany indeed the authorities had long ago made it difficult for Mennonites to claim exemption: this could only be done by hiring a substitute at considerable expense. Some families who could not easily afford to pay such sums emigrated to the United States.

Von Beckerath's position, however, aroused an immediate outcry from the large Old Mennonite communities of West Prussia. Still largely rural, they were more conservative than most Mennonites in other parts of Germany. The statement they issued in reply to von Beckerath's affirmed their united support of nonresistance. Their opposition to military service (which incidentally was still enforced by the imposition of penalties against any who bore arms) was, they stated, "a conviction . . . not to be changed like a piece of clothing." Nevertheless, the defeat of the liberal nationalists, who sought an end to the Mennonites' conscientious exemption in the name of the equality of man, did not terminate the threat which now hung over the heads of the Old Mennonites. In the Prussian diet during the 1850's and 1860's this exemption was challenged by some of the deputies on the same grounds as in 1848.

The crisis arrived in 1867 when, following on Prussia's brief but victorious war against Austria the previous year, the government introduced a new conscription act for the North German Confederation which had just been formed under Prussian hegemony. All able-bodied males were now liable for military service: the act contained no exemption clause for the Mennonites. Remonstrances followed from the leaders of the church, and the king himself assured them that their young men would not be required to violate their consciences. In fact the goverment, when in March 1868 it issued a special order in the matter, was unwilling to concede to the Mennonites more than the right to claim noncombatant duties in the army. They would not have to carry arms, but they would be subject to military discipline on the same conditions as other conscripts. Wearing army uniform, they would be assigned work in military hospitals or as clerks attached to the commissariat.

Consternation ensued as news of these conditions spread among the West Prussian Mennonites. A few diehards urged emigration, which Mennonites had frequently resorted to in times of trouble, rather than submit to the order: in fact, the number of those who left Prussia on this account was very small. A middle group, more numerous than the unconditional nonresistants, advised submitting to the powers that be but at the same time continuing the old policy of disciplining members who volunteered for full military duties. Lastly, there were those who argued in favour of leaving the choice between noncombatant and combatant service to the conscience of each individual to decide. After some hesitation and confusion this was the policy adopted by the church as a whole.

The powerful hold which German nationalism had come to exercise on even the Old Mennonite congregations — apart from a minority who still clung to the old ways — was shown by the wave of patriotic enthusiasm which engulfed them during the Franco-Prussian War of 1870, along with other German Mennonites and the population at large. One of their leading preachers, after praising those heroic German troops who had died to unite the Fatherland, pointed to God's judgement on "the frivolous French" and rejoiced at the return of the Alsatians "to their homeland". In the new *Reich,* although to the end some Mennonite conscripts continued to opt for noncombatant service, their number declined from year to year compared with the number of those who decided to bear arms. "During World War I among the Mennonites killed there were three times as many officers as among the other denominations" (Ernst Crous). In 1934, after Hitler came to power, the church officially gave up its nonresistant stance, which it had already abandoned in practice. There were apparently no Mennonite conscientious objectors in Germany in World War II.

If the Mennonites' peace testimony in Holland and Germany decayed through the absence among church members of a living faith in its efficacy and through the impact on the young of novel ideas from without like democracy and nationalism, most Mennonites in Russia remained attached to nonresistance into the second quarter of the twentieth century. Although there were signs that acculturation was taking place here too — and with similar results as in other sections of the European brotherhood — the process had not gone very far before Stalin's terror during the 1930's and 1940's led to the forced dispersion of the Mennonites, along with suppression of their right to worship freely and to refrain from bearing arms.

We have already seen that Mennonite settlement in the southern plains of the Russian Empire dated to the reign of Catherine II. They remained untroubled in respect to military service for nearly a century. The Empress and the absolute monarchs who succeeded her had promised them exemption from it "for ever." Yet the winds of change were felt even in the Tsarist autocracy. The Mennonites were Germans. So was Catherine II: this did not matter in the cosmopolitan eighteenth century. The Mennonites were pacifists, too. Under the *ancien régime,* we have seen, that did not matter very much either: a clause in their charter of privileges could take care of the problem, so that these useful husbandmen could go happily about their work of colonizing the steppes. But as the nineteenth century progressed, voices were raised in Russia as in the West demanding the integration of alien ethnic groups with the dominant nationality and calling for the destruction of inherited privilege if this was held to conflict with the security of the state. After the Russian defeat in the Crimean War of 1853-1856 the military establishment underwent close scrutiny. Even conservative politicians advocated changes.

34

One of the results of reorganization of the armed forces of the Empire now undertaken in order to make Russia the equal of Western powers like France or Germany was the universal military service act announced in 1870 and made law four years later.

Like the Prussian Mennonites a few years earlier, the Mennonites in Russia seem to have been taken by surprise. The latter, however, had preserved a more lively pacifist tradition. Isolated by their German language and by religion from their Russian and Ukrainian neighbours and with their feeling of community intensified as a result of the virtual autonomy granted their settlements by the Tsarist authorities, they were in a stronger position to resist both cultural and political pressures than the Mennonite churches in either Holland or Germany had been. Therefore, after receiving news that the Russian government now proposed to abolish their "eternal" freedom from service they began to lobby vigorously in St. Petersburg in favour of the existing position and to enlist support from prominent persons in the capital. Meanwhile the brotherhood had become thoroughly alarmed: they were fully conscious of what had just happened to their brethren in Prussia in a similar situation and many of them were determined to leave Russia rather than see their own brotherhood submit to military service, even though of a noncombatant character. For some time indeed the authorities were unprepared to concede more than this last in answer to the Mennonite leaders' expostulations. It was only after they learnt the Mennonites had sent a delegation across the Atlantic to explore the possibilities of settlement there that they began to realize the brotherhood seriously intended to emigrate as a body to North America rather than wear army uniform. Then the government relented. It was loath to lose such excellent citizens whose value to the economy outweighed the fact of their not being Russians and their unwillingness to enter the imperial army. And so in the end it decided to permit Mennonite conscripts to undertake civilian in place of noncombatant military duties, and it set up a Forestry Service, to be run largely by the Mennonites themselves, for this purpose.

The majority of the brotherhood, though they had hoped for better conditions, were ready to agree to this solution. However, over one third of the members — 18,000 out of a total population of 45,000 — found it unsatisfactory and departed for the prairies of Canada or the United States. Accompanying these immigrants were the Hutterite Brethren, who reestablished their communal way of living after arrival in the New World.

The Mennonites who remained in Russia regarded the Forestry Service as on the whole an acceptable compromise. Those who did not had left. It remained in existence until after the outbreak of revolution in 1917 and was dissolved only as a result of the uncertain conditions that then ensued.

During the last half century of the autocracy the Mennonites of Russia began to undergo analogous social changes to those occurring earlier in the Dutch and German brotherhoods. The egalitarian social structure which they possessed at the beginning slowly yielded to one in which class differentiation was increasingly apparent, even if religion and culture still provided a unifying element. Gradually a Mennonite middle class came into being: it was more open to influences from without than the farming brethren were. We shall never know whether, in the normal course of events and as a result mainly of internal factors, the brotherhood in Russia would eventually have abandoned nonresistance along with other aspects of its traditional culture or whether it would have succeeded in finding a fresh basis for them in consonance with the demands of a new age. The communist régime brought it to an abrupt end — not so much because of its principle of nonviolence as because of its German origin, its bourgeois proclivities, and its religious philosophy of life.

The Mennonite emigrants to the New World in the 1870's left Russia chiefly to escape the effects of military conscription, although a desire for new land to develop was not wholly absent from their considerations. On the other hand, those who had left Central Europe between the late seventeenth and the middle of the nineteenth century came to America mainly for economic reasons, although the wish to live in an environment free from the incubus of militarism was not infrequently present, too.

The first Mennonites to settle permanently in North America came in 1683. They chose the recently founded Quaker colony of Pennsylvania for their new home. Here they found unlimited land to cultivate and here, too, they could practice their religion without let or hindrance. In Quaker Pennsylvania no one required them to pay a penalty for refusing to bear arms, and they repaid the Quakers for this by voting for their candidates to the provincial Assembly, which constituted a departure from the usual Mennonite otherworldliness. Living often on the frontier where Whites and Indians mingled they were subject in wartime, however, to the danger of Indian attack. Then their faith in nonviolence was put to the test: we read of families being slaughtered without making resistance. On the whole, though, relations with the native peoples of the new continent were good and the Mennonite farming communities existed peacefully alongside them. In the course of time other small nonresistant groups from Central Europe followed them across the Atlantic: Dunkers who developed into the denomination known today as the Church of the Brethren, Moravians and Schwenkfelders whose founders were German noblemen and whose noncombatancy eventually proved less rigid than the Mennonites' or the Dunkers', as well as Amish whose beliefs and practices were closest to those of the Mennonites.

The Dunkers, though only several hundreds strong at the time of their arrival in the New World in two main groups in 1719 and 1729, were to become in the twentieth century a considerably larger denomination than the Mennonites in the United States. Unlike the Mennonites, however, they had left none of their co-religionists behind in their German homeland. The sect came into being in central Germany in 1708 among Lutheran farmers and artisans who sought a less formal religion than their church then provided. Its founder was a miller, Alexander Mack. There was certainly Mennonite influence on the Dunkers' origins but even stronger was the impact made by certain radical Pietists who sought to restore the way of life of the early church among contemporary Christians. Refusal of military service became from the beginning part of the Dunkers' religious discipline: radical Pietists had pointed to this as an essential element in the apostolic tradition, which the Mennonites strove to exemplify by practising a nonresistant ethic. The same admixture of motives as in the case of the Mennonites prompted the Dunkers to emigrate to North America: a desire for better material conditions combined with the wish to escape both religious persecution and sporadic attempts to force their young men to do military service. In the New World the Dunkers, like the Mennonites, continued for long to be an almost exclusively farming community. With much in common, including their attitude to war, the two sects remained divided on a few issues like the baptismal ritual. (While both practised adult baptism, the Dunkers did this by immersion and the Mennonites by the sprinkling of water.) The early American Dunkers and Mennonites — and the Amish, Moravians and Schwenkfelders, too — all spoke German: for some time none of them encountered any difficulties in maintaining language and culture intact.

The ending of Quaker rule in Pennsylvania and the coming of the American Revolution changed this situation in respect at least to military service, though not too seriously. From 1775 on, religious objectors were required by law to pay a small sum of money in lieu of service in the militia. Similar regulations already prevailed in states like Virginia where for some time now small Mennonite and Dunker congregations existed, too. Since, unlike the Quakers, the German peace sectaries did not object to this procedure for gaining exemption, regarding it as within Caesar's prerogatives to make such demands on them if he wished, no conflicts arose on this score to mar relations with the authorities. We also find Mennonites supplying horses and wagons and acting as civilian drivers for the Revolutionary army. On the other hand, during the Revolution trouble did arise as a result of the Mennonites' unwillingness formally to recognize the new régime when this imposed a compulsory declaration of allegiance. It seemed against their principles to transfer loyalty from the established authority to a rebel power. Fines and sometimes imprisonment and confiscation of property followed from their refusal to take the test or to pay extraordinary taxation imposed by the new authorities. After the conclusion of hostilities suspicion remained in the brotherhood and a group of Mennonites decided to leave the new republic for British territory. They settled in the province of Upper Canada (Ontario today). The majority remained at home where, like the Dunkers, they reverted to the kind of nonconformity to the world they had clung to back in Europe.

'The period between the American Revolution and the American Civil War proved uneventful in so far as Mennonite nonresistance is concerned. Their young men paid their militia fines and went about their business. The discipline was applied as a matter of course to the few who bore arms, and expulsion was the fate of any who remained recalcitrant. The same pattern prevailed, too, among the Dunkers. By the middle of the nineteenth century the state militias were in decay: service in any case had become a formality. The authorities scarcely gave a thought to the conscientious objection of their German speaking peace sects.

And these sects themselves proved scarcely interested in exploring the implications of their heritage of nonresistance, provided their members observed the letter of the tradition. They published little on the subject to guide those in doubt: their young people received scant instruction as to what the practice of nonviolence really meant. For Mennonites and Dunkers alike "the period prior to the Civil War was a period of spiritual decline" (Guy F. Hershberger). This decline resulted in large part from the cultural isolation in which these churches now lived. True, such isolation protected them from the corrosive influence of a secular and nonpacifist environment, as exercised, for instance, in the case of the Dutch Mennonites. But it carried other dangers. Westward migration strengthened the spiritual barriers which these sects, consisting almost exclusively of farming folk and lacking a trained ministry, had already erected against the outside world. Congregations living on the new frontier were left to their own cultural resources: the ingrained conservatism they had originally carried with them from Europe brought about a fossilization of Mennonite and Dunker ideology which has only been overcome in our century. Though pious, simple and sincere, the average Mennonite or Dunker farmer possessed a faith that was narrow, rigid, and legalistic. The living spirit had left it. This spirit no longer inspired its pacifism, either.

Thus the two churches were ill equipped to deal with the situation created by the outbreak of war between North and South in 1861. In the North, many of their young men, finding their ancestral creed inadequate, left to join the Unionist army. This happened even among the Amish among whom nonconformity to the world was strictest. (However in the South, opposition to the institution of slavery precluded any martial enthusiasm.) The majority of Mennonites and Dunkers who were of military age, however, claimed the status of conscientious objector.

Lincoln's administration was not wholly unsympathetic to this position. In fact, for most of the war all that needed to be done to gain exemption was to produce a certificate of peace church membership and pay the sum of $300. The poorer members of a congregation were helped by their better off brethren to find the money. On the other hand, for the period of a year from March 1863 to February 1864, when older legislation had lapsed and new provisions for religious objectors had not yet been promulgated, the only possibility of exemption was to hire a substitute. Mennonites did this but, as always, with a bad conscience. In addition, there were young men who shared their church's belief in nonresistance but, though liable to the call-up, were not yet of an age to receive baptism, the outward symbol of acceptance into membership. Since they could not produce a membership certificate these people were forced, too, to resort to the hiring of a substitute if they wished to escape induction into the army. Those who bore arms either as volunteers or as conscripts were usually disfellowshipped, although the discipline was no longer applied with the vigour of former days.

The situation of the Mennonites and Dunkers who lived in the Confederate States, mainly in Virginia, was much less happy than the lot of their Northern brethren. They were known to be antislavery people and opposed to secession, and this did not endear them to the authorities. However, there were prominent government officials on the Confederate side, too, who understood and respected the churches' nonbelligerent stand and worked to get legislation passed granting them exemption from military service on terms they could accept honourably. And even General "Stonewall" Jackson thought it better to leave them at home where they would produce foodstuffs which could be used by the Confederate army rather than to force them to become unwilling — as well as inefficient — soldiers. But eighteen months elapsed from the start of hostilities before a law was passed which gave the peace sectaries the option of paying a commutation fee (the sum demanded — $500 — was rather high).

Before this date their conscientious objectors had encountered many hardships. True, they might resort to hiring a substitute: this, we know, was then a way out open to anyone with the means to pay. But the Mennonite and Dunkers of Virginia were almost all indigent farmers: few of them, especially when they had large families, could afford to do this, for the price set for a substitute might run to as much as $1,500. Besides, the practice was frowned on by their churches. Thus in the early months of the war we find many of their young men accepting induction into the army with the determination not to shoot even if ordered to do so. Usually their officers were at least vaguely acquainted with the background of these men and knew that their unwillingness to take human life stemmed from their religion: they tried to assign them, therefore, to various noncombatant duties as drivers or kitchen orderlies or nurses. Then at the earliest opportunity they got permission to send them back on an indefinite furlough to their farms. Sometimes the men just left on their own without waiting for leave. There were other young Mennonites and Dunkers who went into hiding, emerging again only after legal exemption had been granted them. Several groups attempted to escape to the North but were intercepted on their way and interned, until released as a result of the efforts of their churches' leaders, who persuaded the authorities the men were not actively disloyal. In the last weeks of the war a shortage of manpower led the Confederate Congress to pass a more stringent military service act: it contained no provision for the exemption of religious objectors. If hostilities had not soon come to an end, therefore, the Southern peace sectaries might have had to face a period of renewed persecution for their pacifist beliefs.

Their behaviour during wartime, though consistently nonresistant, had been marked by hesitation and confusion as to the form their peace witness should take. Unlettered ploughboys and simple farmers were then faced with making decisions for which their previous experience had provided scant guidance. Their churches produced a few energetic and articulate leaders capable of arguing their case before Confederate officialdom. But this fact could not replace the need for a fundamental rethinking of their position that would put nonresistance on a strong enough basis to cope with the realities of the modern world. On the Unionist side, where Mennonites and Dunkers faced a less hostile state and society and where from the beginning their conscientious scruples about fighting were respected by the government, their peace testimony was basically in no more healthy a state than in the South. The size of the minority who opted for active service instead of the traditional noncombatancy gave an indication that something was amiss here.

Renewal was slow in coming, slower indeed among the Dunkers than among the Mennonites. The influx in the 1870's of Mennonites from Russia, who had chosen to leave their own country rather than compromise on the issue of war, helped to some extent to reinvigorate their North American coreligionists' witness for peace. Some attempt was now being made to give instruction, even if inadequate, on questions of peace and war. Pamphlets and articles in the church press were now being published on the subject, and the first signs appeared of willingness to collaborate with other peace people in the struggle against war. The North American Mennonites, like the Dunkers, remained for some time an overwhelmingly rural sect which continued to stand aloof from politics or close contact with other sections of the nation. But in the twentieth century the old way of life of both peace churches began to change. Mennonites and Dunkers moved into the city; they started to attend college and university; they often shared now the same cultural interests and aspirations as their neighbours of other — or no — religious persuasion. Some sections of their brotherhoods clung desperately to the ancient paths and attempted to maintain their rural isolation in face of the advance of urban civilization. Others tried to save only what they considered to be the essentials of the tradition and were ready to abandon the German language and the plain dress and the unyielding refusal to participate in even the positive aspects of government. These things, they argued, must go anyhow, the victims of the inevitable — and not necessarily harmful — process of acculturation. Twentieth-century Mennonites have sought to recover the vision of the sixteenth-century Anabaptists and make it meaningful in a vastly changed environment. At the centre of this vision as their scholars have reinterpreted it for them stands the principle of nonresistance*. It is too early yet to say whether Mennonites and Dunkers in the New World will succeed in maintaining their traditional identity by giving fresh life to old concepts or whether, as happened with the Mennonites in the Netherlands and Germany, they will eventually integrate fully with society and discard their traditional testimonies, including nonresistance.

---

*Recent historical reinterpretations by Mennonite scholars include: John H. Yoder, " 'Anabaptists and the Sword' Revisited: Systematic Historiography and Undogmatic Nonresistants," *Zeitschrift für Kirchengeschichte* (Stuttgart), vol. LXXXV (1974), no. 2, pp. 126 [270] - 139 [283], and H.-J. Goertz, *Die Täufer: Geschichte und Deutung* (Munich, 1980), pp. 113-24.

3. THE QUAKER PEACE TESTIMONY TO WORLD WAR I

(a) *The Era of Fox and Penn*

In England the middle decades of the seventeenth century when Quakerism emerged were marked by war and theological strife. The Anabaptist-Mennonite movement on the continent had arisen under somewhat similar conditions in the second quarter of the previous century. The question has been debated by scholars whether Quakerism's birth resulted in part from the influence of the earlier movement, or whether certain similarities in doctrine — such as their common opposition to participation in war — were not merely coincidental and whether Quakerism was not purely an outcome, however irregular, of the English Puritanism that also produced Oliver Cromwell. A recent historian (belonging to the American Church of the Brethren) has argued persuasively in favour of some indirect influence from Mennonites as well as mystics on the continent, even though Quakerism's immediate origins must clearly be sought within the left wing of Puritanism.

The Quakers were not the first British group to declare their adherence to pacifism. Some of the Lollards, followers of the Oxford reformer John Wyclif who had died in 1384, carried their master's conditional opposition to war one step further and expressed their unwillingness "to fight bodily", declaring "that manslaughter by battle or ... law ... is express contrarious to the New Testament." But how many of the sect took this position and how long those who did so continued to maintain it is unclear. Due to severe persecution the Lollards had virtually disappeared before the Reformation. However, in the sixteenth century Anabaptism spread from the Netherlands to England. In 1563 the Church of England when it drew up its Thirty-Nine Articles devoted a sentence to refuting that sect's nonresistance. "It is lawful", we read in the thirty-seventh article, "for Christian men, at the commandment of the magistrate, to wear weapons and serve in the wars." Yet Anabaptism, while it gained some converts, never made much headway in England. It merged towards the end of the sixteenth century with the wider separatist movement which gave birth to England's first nonconformist churches — the Congregationalists and the Baptists. There was undoubtedly some Mennonite influence on the earliest stage of the English Baptist movement. Both groups, for instance, advocated adult baptism in contrast to all other Christian churches. Some English Baptists adopted the idea of nonresistance, too, and a few may have persisted in holding antimilitarist sentiments down to the time of the English Civil War.

Despite the possible existence of peripheral influences from Anabaptist and Mennonite sources, the Quaker peace testimony, when it appeared during the Commonwealth period, was nevertheless a rediscovery of pacifism, virtually a new beginning and not the continuation of an earlier chapter in pacifist history. Indeed emergent Quakerism reached a pacifist position only after considerable wrestling of the spirit and after many hesitations and some backsliding.

The prophetic cobbler, George Fox, rightly considered the founder of Quakerism, first began to gather followers around the year 1650. These were mostly seekers after religious truth who had failed to find what they were looking for in the various sects of that time. The new faith originated in the Midlands and soon spread to the rest of England and Wales and then to Calvinist Scotland and troubled Ireland. From 1656 on it began to take root across the Atlantic in the American colonies stretched out along the Eastern seaboard. Precarious Quaker communities were established, too, in many of the islands of the West Indies as well as on the European continent in Dutch- and German-speaking lands. What attracted newcomers in Fox's message was the belief that each individual, through the guidance of the Inner Light, could follow righteousness and win understanding of God's will for man without the intermediacy of priesthood or pastorate. According to Quakers, even the Bible, though worthy of reverence for the divine teaching in contained, was not the most essential instrument of salvation. Fox and his disciples rejected the ancient doctrine of the depravity of man: mankind, they held, might win redemption through the Light set by God within every human being. Early Quakers expected they would win the world for their beliefs, and engaged therefore with truly extraordinary energy in what they called the Lamb's War to bring this conversion about. George Fox, who possessed a talent for organization at least equal to his charismatic gift, realized the need to provide institutional channels for directing and controlling the outpourings of the Holy Spirit and eventually established a Society of Friends (as Quakers liked to call themselves) based on preparatory meetings at the grassroots and reaching up to the executive Meeting for Sufferings at the top. This democratic pattern was adopted by Quakers overseas and adapted to their differing circumstances.

At first the question of peace did not figure very prominently among the concerns of Fox and his Friends. Their endeavours were concentrated chiefly upon proclaiming the Truth and spreading their message throughout Christendom: an attempt was even made to take it to the Muslim world. At first indeed protest against the payment of tithes or against the imposition of official oaths appears to have been more important to them than the repudiation of violence and warfare. The peace testimony as a collective witness against war emerged gradually: it did not spring from any sudden revelation on the part of Fox or any of his followers. Fox himself came early to the conclusion that, as a warrior in the Lamb's War, he must abandon "carnal weapons." In the autumn of 1650 we find him telling Cromwell's officers who were offering him the rank of captain in the militia that he now "lived in the virtue of that life and power that took away the occasion of all wars" and that he "was come into the covenant of peace which was before wars and strifes" were. "I told them", he relates in his *Journal,* "I was brought off from outward wars." In these statements, as indeed in most of his utterances on war, Fox appeals to its incompatability with the Christian spirit and with the Light within man which reflects this rather than to any New Testament text. Not law, which formed the core of Mennonite nonresistance, but spirit remained the basis of the Quaker peace testimony, at least until the impact of evangelicalism much later upon the Society of Friends. In the striking words of James Nayler (Fox's contemporary who shared his prophetic voice but lacked, however, his plain common sense) this spirit strives "to outlive all wrath and contention and to weary out all exaltation and cruelty, or whatever is of a nature contrary to itself . . . If it be betrayed, it bears it; for its ground and spring are the mercies and forgiveness of God. Its crown is meekness, its life is everlasting love unfeigned."

But not all the early Quakers were meek, even if only in spirit, nor did they always remain content merely to outlive the wrath of the godless. Among them at the beginning there were militant republicans, Commonwealth army men, devoted supporters of the Good Old Cause. Moreover, Fox himself, for all his personal belief in nonviolence, did not see fit at this time to urge them, once they had thrown in their lot with the Quaker movement, to leave their profession of arms on pacifist grounds. Although they were all dismissed eventually from the forces or left voluntarily, this happened usually for reasons unconnected with opposition to war: its source lay in these Quaker soldiers' increasing disillusionment with the régime's declining republican zeal. In 1659 when an opportunity seemed to open up for the establishment of a leftwing republican government, a number of Friends accepted military office. Even Fox seems to have had a period of doubt, from which, however, he emerged more confident even than before in the rightness of his stand against all forms of violence. "Fighters are not of Christ's kingdom, but are without Christ's kingdom", he concluded.

With respect to the first decade of Quakerism it is difficult to uncover exactly the stages of the peace testimony's growth. Throughout these years Fox in his preaching and writing proclaimed his message of peace. The Inner Light, he declared, "leads out of wars, leads out of strife, leads out of the occasion of wars." It would impel those who still clung to war as an instrument for accomplishing righteousness finally to renounce all but spiritual weapons. And indeed, before the *débâcle* of republican hopes in 1659 and again in 1660, the year in which Charles II at last returned to claim his kingdoms when even the Quaker militants ungirt their swords and adopted the meek stance of the Lamb, many Friends had already absorbed Fox's message of nonviolence. Well before these dates we know of some Quaker soldiers in Cromwell's army who, after their conversion, "purposed not to make use of any carnal sword" as well as of a few Quaker sailors in the Commonwealth navy who refused to fight. "The developing peace testimony", writes Kenneth L. Carroll, "was the 'clincher' which brought about the disappearance of Quakerism in the Cromwellian Army in Ireland even before the end of the Commonwealth and the Protectorate." Certainly by 1659, and probably before that date, there were already Quaker conscientious objectors to service in the county militias. In 1658 a case of conscientious objection is recorded from Maryland, and if opposition to military service already existed among Quakers on the other side of the Atlantic, it is likely the sentiment had become widespread in Quakerism's British homeland still earlier. Therefore, the thesis propounded recently by several writers that the Quakers' pacifism was a "post-revolutionary" product, a reaction stemming from their disappointment at the destruction of their hopes for the establishment of a republic of the Saints, cannot be accepted without considerable qualification. However much it may apply to one section of the Society, it certainly cannot be fitted to the whole Quaker community.

The Restoration coincided with, and to some extent caused, a consolidation of Quakerism behind its peace testimony. This took final shape in a *Declaration from the Harmless and Innocent People of God called Quakers,* which Fox and his colleagues issued in January 1661 as their "testimony to the whole world". The statement was published for the purpose of disassociating Friends from the abortive plot to overthrow Charles II's rule, which the republican Fifth Monarchy Men had then attempted: the authors of the declaration intended to make clear that Quakers were precluded by their principles from taking part in any kind of armed action. "The Spirit of Christ, by which we are guided", it stated, "is not changeable, so as once to command us from a thing as evil, and again to move us to it, and we certainly know and do testify to the world, that the Spirit of Christ . . . will never move us to fight and war against any man with outward weapons, neither for the Kingdom of Christ nor the kingdoms of this world."

Fox remained the prophet and missionary. The task of elaborating and refining the Quaker faith fell to a learned Scotsman, Robert Barclay, whose *Apology* first appeared (in Latin) in 1676. In his writings on peace Barclay, while he continues to emphasize the contradiction between Christian love and carnal fighting, dwells, too, on the destructive powers of war and the desirability of achieving international peace. This was something new in the history of pacifism. The Anabaptists and Mennonites, we have seen, despaired of this world, and even Fox and the first generation of Quakers omitted pragmatic considerations altogether in their condemnation of war. The search for means of implementing

Quaker pacifism on an international scale, which begins with Barclay, was carried further by William Penn, the admiral's son and Oxford graduate, who had joined Friends in 1667. Penn, while he shared the principled Quaker objection to war, was also concerned to discover ways of decreasing the incidence of war between the nations. In his *Essay towards the Present and Future Peace of Europe* of 1693 he followed in the footsteps of the French statesman, the duc de Sully, and proposed the establishment of an embryo league of nations to maintain peace. Since Penn in drawing up his plan presumed the nations had not become converts to Quaker pacifism, he provided for the employment of military sanctions in the last resort in case efforts at imposing arbitration on the contending parties failed.

We cannot easily conceive of a plan of this sort — which of course did not represent Penn's ideal solution — emanating from Menno or even Fox. Early Quaker pacifists, while they regarded the magistracy as essential for human welfare, tended to take the position of the Anabaptist-Mennonite nonresistants and doubt if a true follower of Christ could hold official office because of its inevitable connection with the sword. Only later did Quakers begin to make a clear distinction on the one hand between those aspects of the magistracy associated with war-making, and on the other its police functions, participation in which seemed to them now to be admissible. For war aimed at the indiscriminate destruction of human beings, whereas police action sought to discriminate between guilty and innocent and to preserve rather than destroy human personality. Penn, for example, regarded the magistracy as "both lawful and useful" (as he told the King of Poland).

Penn indeed, by attempting to give broader political expression to the Quaker peace testimony, "established the humanitarian tradition in the work of Friends" (Wolf Mendl). His fame as a politician is chiefly associated with the founding of Pennsylvania, whose charter he received from the king's hands in 1682. Quaker rule over the province lasted until 1756, a total of seventy-four years. Penn's main object in settling his new province was to provide a place of refuge for his sorely tried coreligionists. For the new sect the reigns of Charles II and his brother, James II, despite the two monarchs' not entirely unfriendly attitude, constituted a period of severe persecution. For most of the time Quakers had had to face heavy fines and imprisonment, ill-treatment by the mob as well as the breaking up of their religious meetings. This had not prevented them either from spreading their faith far and wide or from creating a disciplined organization in the mother country and then transplanting it overseas. But when freedom of religious worship finally came, first with the Declaration of Indulgence promulgated a year before, and then the Act of Toleration a year after, the Glorious Revolution of 1688, the Society was suffering to some extent from exhaustion; something of the original fire had gone from its spiritual life.

Conceived in the period of persecution and at a time when Quaker religion was still vigorous, Pennsylvania in the mind of its founder was seen both as a haven for harried Friends and a model society in which these newcomers could put into practice their belief in nonviolence. Justice and peace would become the watchwords of Quaker government.

The long period of Quaker rule in Pennsylvania which followed fulfilled in part the high hopes of its founder and its first settlers, who aspired to the creation of a "holy experiment" within the boundaries of the new colony. Pennsylvania remained virtually unarmed for some seven decades. During this time no citizen of the province was ever required to bear weapons: Quakers and indeed all others remained free to pursue the ways of peace, if they so wished. Moreover, beginning with Penn himself and for many years to come a serious attempt was made to deal justly with the indigenous Indians with whom the settlers came into contact.

Despite the warlike character of some of these tribes, the province was for long exempt from the fierce and merciless frontier warfare which plagued the other American colonies. It was Penn's earnest wish that Quakers and Indians should dwell alongside each other "as neighbours and friends." And in fact it was not until after his death that relations between white and red man began to deteriorate. In addition, the penal code of Quaker Pennsylvania, although it might seem harsh today, "was remarkable for its humaneness, especially as it existed side by side with codes loaded down with atrocious sanctions" (Lawrence H. Gipson).

Yet the holy experiment, while partly successful for a time, suffered from various tensions between the principle of Quaker nonviolence, which Penn sought to exemplify in his colony, and the fact of its political subordination to a nonpacifist government at home. These tensions were to shake the foundations of Quaker rule so that eventually it collapsed. A certain ambivalence in Penn's position existed indeed from the outset. The royal charter which granted the colony to him and his heirs bestowed the rank of "Captain-General" on the proprietor. In the eyes of the home government Pennsylvania had to take its place within the framework of transatlantic imperial strategy: its defense in wartime was linked with that of the other North American colonies, for whom — as for London — pacifism was scarcely intelligible as a practical policy. Since Penn visited his colony only at rare intervals — he was fully engaged in Quaker work in Britain — in his absence his place was taken by a deputy-governor who wielded the highest executive authority in the colony. Whereas for the first few years Penn appointed prominent Quakers to this office, he soon abandoned this practice and he and his heirs nominated only military men. "Being not a Friend", wrote Penn of his appointee of 1688, an army captain, he "could deal with those that were not and stop their mouths, and be stiff with neighbours on occasion. This was my motive to have him." Penn feared, too, that the Crown might deprive him of the province and that the position of Pennsylvania Quakers would thus be endangered, if some solution were not found in respect to military affairs that would prove reasonably satisfactory to the authorities in London. The army officers, appointed successively to the deputy-governorship by Penn and his heirs, seldom, however, enjoyed good relations with the Quakers of Pennsylvania.

We see here a willingness to compromise on Penn's part that some otherwise sympathetic historians have severely criticized, accusing him of displaying a lack of sincerity and openness in his dealings. "We must creep where we cannot go", Penn told Pennsylvania Quakers on one occasion, "and it is as necessary for us, in the things of life, to be wise as to be innocent." On another occasion, after having succeeded in resisting pressure to establish a provincial militia, he acquiesced in the posting of an armed ship at the mouth of the Delaware river to ward off attack by pirates or other enemies. "By sea", wrote Penn while explaining why there was no need for a militia on land, "a small vessel of war would, under God's providence, be the best security".

A similar lack of reluctance to stand on the letter of pacifist consistency is found in the Quaker politicians who controlled the provincial assembly. The home government, especially in wartime, presented that body on occasions with demands for financial aid to support its military operations. The assemblymen were reluctant to make war appropriations of this kind, at any rate directly. In the 1690's, during "King William's War" against Louis XIV, a formula was devised that salved Quaker consciences, at least for some time to come.

Henceforward, though usually only after considerable bickering between assembly and deputy-governor, a sum of money was granted for the monarch's "use" — "as a token of our duty" (to cite the phrase used by the assembly in

1711 during Queen Anne's reign). What was thereafter done with it was not considered to be Friends' business: "*that* being not our part, but hers", said a leading Quaker assemblyman on this occasion. This position, it should be pointed out, was not without its own inner logic. "For the Quakers the formula . . . represents both the maintenance of the peace testimony and the fulfilment of their duty as subjects" (Hermann Wellenreuther). The English crown, in their view, had the obligation to protect its citizens by arms — until the time should come when Quaker principles of peace had become universal. Meanwhile Quakers, faithfully observing their resolution not to fight with worldly weapons, must at the same time carry out loyally their obligations to their ruler up to the point where such obligations conflicted with their prior duty towards God. In this period, apart from one querulous pamphleteer driven, it would seem, more by party strife and personal ambition than by Quaker principle, Pennsylvania Quakers on the whole do not appear to have seriously contested this viewpoint.

In addition to the fatal entanglement of the pacifist colony in the power politics of the mother country another basic reason for the ultimate failure of the holy experiment lay in the political and social structure of Quaker Pennsylvania. In the first place, we see the growth of party politics which divided the Quaker community and disturbed its peaceful development. Bitter strife arose between the constitutionalists and the conservatives. Leaders and rank and file of both parties were drawn for the most part from members of the Society of Friends. While on the one hand the ferment thus created witnessed to the vitality of political life in the province, on the other hand it became increasingly clear that "to the political Quakers the struggle for power meant more than the cause of peace" (Guy F. Hershberger). It was more and more difficult, too, for the wealthy Quaker merchants of Philadelphia, however much they strove to preserve the plain living of their ancestors, to observe their Society's peace testimony with proper exactitude when pacifism conflicted with their business interests. Moreover, just as political conflict threatened to destroy the unity of Quaker meetings, the considerable differences which had now appeared in the economic situation of the membership furnished yet another factor which retarded the achievement of the goals of the holy experiment. A Philadelphia grandee who could often retire to live as a country gentleman did not have too much in common, beyond membership of the same religious Society, with a simple Quaker farmer toiling on his small plot of land in the back country. More serious from the point of view of Pennsylvania's pacifism was the fact that the Quakers, while continuing to dominate both the executive and the legislature by means of an antiquated franchise no longer consonant with the demographic map, soon ceased to form a majority of the province's inhabitants. True, many of the new immigrants were German sectaries, some of them more rigidly nonresistant than the Quakers themselves and all of them anxious only to worship freely as they wished and cultivate the soil exempt from the burdens imposed by a militaristic state. But a considerable section of the newcomers, the so-called "Scotch-Irish", for instance, did not have any sympathy with the Quaker attitude on war. They were kept from having their due say in political life only by means of the electoral geometry practised by the Quaker establishment.

Finally, we may mention as an element undermining the attempt made in Pennsylvania to set up a pacifist commonwealth the fact that certain influential members of the Society no longer shared its belief in nonviolence. There were the two Isaac Norrises, for instance, and James Logan, who had been William Penn's private secretary for a number of years. The Quaker nonpacifists formed a small minority within the Society and they did not attempt openly to attack the peace testimony. But some of them held important positions inside the province's political power structure: later they formed the nucleus of the so-called Quaker Party which continued to rule Pennsylvania after the Society of Friends had officially withdrawn from participation in political life.

Whatever the shortcomings of the Pennsylvania experiment and however much it eventually deviated from the pacifist model Penn and the first Quaker settlers had envisaged, the Quaker colony right up to the outbreak of the American Revolution shielded its citizens from the burden of military conscription which weighed on Friends elsewhere in North America as well as in Great Britain and on the European continent. Only in Rhode Island, whose government was controlled by Quakers virtually without a break from 1663 to 1714, were conditions almost as favourable to the conscientious objector as in Pennsylvania. Here an act of 1673 granted complete exemption from military duties to all genuine religious objectors. Only if enemy invasion were imminent would they be required to perform some kind of civilian service: "works of mercy manifested to distressed, weak persons." This legislation represents the first British grant of exemption from military service to persons holding pacifist views.

Outside Quaker Pennsylvania and semi-Quaker Rhode Island everywhere the Friend who was both male and ablebodied faced a number of problems posed by his Society's — and presumably his own — objection to bearing arms. In the first place there was the statutory obligation, enforced fairly regularly at this period both in Great Britain and overseas, to perform service in the local militia. At times of danger — which was fairly often in areas like the West Indies where invasion remained an ever present threat — Quakers might be required, along with their fellow citizens, to watch with arms to prevent disturbances of the peace or to forestall an expected enemy attack. In coastal areas on both sides of the Atlantic the press gang roamed the ports in search of lusty young fellows to man the royal navy: from time to time they would seize upon an unwary Quaker. Early in the Society's history the problem of alternative service had to be grappled with, too. Which alternatives to personal service with arms were acceptable and which must be rejected?

In regard to militia service, the most frequently recurring demand made by the authorities, a pattern of required behaviour developed fairly soon among Friends. His Society expected the objector not merely of course to refuse to serve personally. He was forbidden as well either to hire a substitute, an alternative open at that time to all draftees including those not opposed on principle to bearing arms, or to pay the fine — often quite small — which was the legal penalty for nonappearance at the place of muster. Refusal to pay usually entailed distraint of goods, often to a value considerably higher than the original militia fine, or imprisonment for some weeks or months, if the objector possessed insufficient property on which to levy a distraint.

This procedure ensued on both sides of the Atlantic wherever militia conscription and Quaker community were found together. The Quaker objection to accepting a monetary commutation in exchange for service in person, a way out of difficulty which, we have seen, Mennonites were able conscientiously to follow, stemmed from the Society's unwillingness to see its members voluntarily paying a penalty for conduct they considered to be morally right. (Quakers after all — both at home and in North America — were proud of being free-born Englishmen: a sentiment which a Central European Mennonite farmer might find hard to comprehend.) Payment of the fine, therefore, appeared tantamount to admission of wrongdong: disciplinary action by his local meeting might result if the objector yielded on this point. The militia "sufferings" of Friends were all carefully noted in the Society's records as were the occasions when a member failed to "suffer . . . for truth." Only in the West Indies were harsher penalties not infrequently meted out to Quaker objectors. Here we read from time to time of heavy fines and lengthy imprisonment as well as severe physical ill-treatment. Difficulties in maintaining their stand *vis-à-vis* military service constituted one of the factors leading to the decline and eventual extinction of Quakerism in the British West Indies. The same factor was at work, too, in preventing the growth of the Society on the European continent first among the Dutch and Germans and then in the eighteenth century among the French: the political environment there was hostile to the kind of uncompromising peace witness professed by Friends. This could flourish in practice only in polities influenced by the libertarian tradition which had emerged in seventeenth-century England.

British Quakers do not seem to have objected to paying towards the maintenance of the town watch, even though its members might have to carry arms, a fact that would prevent Friends from participating personally. This position, however, did not appear to be as clear when viewed by Friends in the islands of the pirate infested Caribbean Sea as it was in England. In the Caribbean islands Quaker practice varied. In Barbados, for instance, Friends participated personally — but unarmed — "in watching, and warding, and patrolling", when there were fears of a Black slave uprising. (Overseas Quakers, we may note, rid themselves of the taint of slaveholding only in the course of the eighteenth century.) On the other hand, we find Friends on Nevis at this time raising doubts concerning the compatability with the peace testimony of Friends watching, even without arms. Even assurances from George Fox himself that the practice was indeed Quakerly did not put their minds at rest, and most of them continued to refuse this duty. "They will neither watch nor ward", reported the governor of the island indignantly.

If Friends were uncertain in the matter of watching and warding, they entertained no doubts concerning right behaviour in case of impressment into the Royal Navy. There were many Quaker mariners in this period, drawn chiefly from the coastal meetings, and there were Quaker shipowners, too, whose vessels plied the Atlantic Ocean as well as other seas. Both sailor and entrepreneur were expected to prove their loyalty to peace principles, the one by refusing to serve on armed ships and the other by refraining from providing with guns the boats he owned, either in part or in whole. For neither party was the way easy, for in those days most ships carried armament for use against pirates and other marauders, and in wartime against the enemy. Eventual disownment was normally the fate of one who defied his Society's discipline on this point. However, we should add, it proved not too difficult for a wealthy Quaker merchant to conceal the entanglement of his business with armed enterprises of this sort. In the eighteenth century even weighty Friends in London or Philadelphia were sometimes guilty of such double dealing: a reflection of the declining moral fervour of the Society as a whole. Service in the fighting fleet, on the other hand, was clearly contrary to the Quaker ethos. Considerable effort was expended by the Society in freeing members from captivity after impressment; during their forcible detainment in the capacity of jack-tars these men had often to undergo rough treatment and manhandling. We possess firsthand accounts of their experiences by Quakers taken up by the press-gang, all of them simple men whose artless narratives retain the genuine ring of truth. Sometimes the navy freed such men without further ado, not wishing to have trouble on their hands. "Turn him away, he is a Quaker", said the captain of a seventeenth-century man-of-war hastily when confronted with Friend Thomas Lurting whom the press-gang had just landed on his deck.

Alternative service was not a usual option for seventeenth- or eighteenth-century Quaker objectors. But it was offered by the authorities in the New World on several occasions. As in the case of watching, Friends did not give a united answer as to whether acceptance of service of this kind in lieu of bearing arms was permissible. True, to undertake under such conditions noncombatant work of a military character — for example, constructing ramparts or fortifications or driving wagons for army use — was not allowed. But what of other duties where the connection with war was less direct? In 1705, when there was serious danger of a French attack by sea, Friends on the island of Antigua were exempted from bearing arms on condition they undertook seemingly innocuous labour on "building . . . watch-houses, clearing common roads, making bridges, digging ponds", etc. The older members of the meeting strongly favoured compliance; the younger ones disagreed and could see no difference between carrying out work like this, which was designed to aid the island's military defense, and accepting combatant service. At best, they said, it would be to do "a lawful thing upon an unlawful account and bottom." Advice was sought from London Yearly Meeting which enjoyed immense prestige throughout the whole Society of Friends. The leaders of English Quakerism, who included the late George Fox's son-in-law, in a letter displaying excessive caution came out decisively against the radical stand of the young Antiguan Quakers. They could see no good reason why the authorities' generosity in offering useful work should be rejected. And they discounted the young men's argument that it was indistinguishable in kind from full military duties. (London Friends' standpoint, we may note, was scarcely compatible with the Society's absolutist position with respect to the nonpayment of militia fines.)

The question of alternative service merges with the wider problem of war work in general, with which Quaker men of all ages might have to cope in this period. This could present even more delicate issues for solution. The Hutterites, we have seen, adamantly refused to undertake any work which they knew would contribute to the waging of war. (They refused to perform even genuinely noncombatant service if offered as an alternative to fighting.) Quakers seem to have been less consistent, at least in the seventeenth century — without being able to plead the same rationale for compliance the Mennonites could do. In this area the Quaker conscience appears not to have awakened so quickly to the implications of behaviour as in the case of its members' militia obligations. We find, for instance, Quaker craftsmen towards the end of the seventeenth century working in the naval shipyard at Chatham: they were not, it would appear, brought to book by the Society for helping to construct men-of-war. However, insufficient evidence is available at present to form a definitive judgement on the Quaker position.

We know more about the Society's official stance in regard to war taxes. Members were admonished to withhold payment of a straight militia rate, obviously destined for the upkeep of that institution. They could be disciplined, too, for yielding to the authorities' demands to pay "Trophy Money" and other imposts of like nature (as they could for closing their shops during days of mourning for military defeats or illuminating their houses during celebrations of victories). Nonconformity to these demands symbolized Quaker opposition to war and organized violence. On the other hand, Friends agreed they must pay without murmuring all taxes "in the mixture", that is, where the proportions allotted by government respectively to civil and military uses were impossible to determine. For the magistracy was divinely appointed: its proper functioning depended on its subjects rendering it tribute regularly. "I make a distinction", declared a London Quaker in 1679, "between the military power and the civil. The military power's command is, Go, fire, kill and destroy. The civil power's command is, Go, keep the peace" (from *Fellowship*, 1 May 1960). Paying ordinary taxes, Quakers felt, was but doing their duty as citizens and did not constitute a dereliction of their peace testimony. The Society's attitude towards extraordinary taxation clearly destined for military purposes was, however, more ambiguous. If a specific military object for collecting the tax, e.g. the construction of fortifications or the provision of arms, was known to exist, Friends sometimes balked at paying. But during England's wars against the Dutch and French, Fox himself paid special taxes levied for carrying on hostilities and told his followers to do likewise. "To the earthly we give the earthly", he explained, "that is, to Caesar we give unto him his things, and to God we give unto Him His things." The Quaker legislators of Pennsylvania, we have seen, took the same attitude. And in this they received the warm support of English Friends. It was the subject's obligation to give, most Friends seem to have agreed, and the ruler's right to choose how he would apply the tribute rendered to him.

The Quaker witness for peace in this period had to a large extent to be expressed in negative terms: objection to military service, resistance to impressment, refusal to arm vessels, etc. There was, of course, the holy experiment, the attempt to set up a "peaceable kingdom" to act as a model of the way men could live without weapons. And Friends, in their dealings with the American Indians, tried, too, to exemplify the ideal of nonviolence. Apart from Barclay and Penn, however, there were as yet only a handful of Quakers concerned to work out the implications of their Society's peace testimony for international relations.

Penn lived on until 1718, though in 1712 a stroke had totally incapacitated him from transacting business. Barclay had died in 1690, and the founder of Quakerism, George Fox, followed him to the grave the next year. By now the Society of Friends had won religious toleration along with other dissenting sects, though they were still excluded in Great Britain from participation in political life. Across the Atlantic, however, the Society ruled Pennsylvania and constituted an important factor in the politics of Rhode Island. The heroic age in its history had passed. God fearing, industrious, frugal and conscientious, the average Quaker was now generally respected by his fellow citizens, who were usually prepared to put up with his peculiar objections to bearing arms, taking an oath and doffing his hat and with his use of the second person in address. The flame of the Society's spiritual life had died down, though it was never entirely extinguished. A stillness had fallen on its meetings: it was sometimes difficult to know if this stemmed from intensity of meditation or from mental torpor. The era of quietism had now begun when Friends feared to break the silence of their worship lest the cares of the world should break in.

(b) *Quietism and Revolution*

Tradition dominated the peace witness of Quakers during the eighteenth century as it dominated most other aspects of the life of the Society of Friends in that period. At first this was as true of Friends in the New World as of those who remained in the British Isles. But two events occurring in the third quarter of the century shook the Quakers of the American colonies and reshaped their pacifism as well as their whole attitude to state and society. The first event in point of time was the movement of internal renewal initiated in the 1750's by a group of concerned Friends centred in Philadelphia Yearly Meeting, the second was the outbreak in 1775 of an eventually successful insurrection against the mother country. The first brought the holy experiment in Pennsylvania to a close, the second caused American Quakerism as a whole to withdraw within itself and eschew political action for almost a century. As a consequence of the renewal it had experienced, American Quakerism came for a time to display a fresher, more lively, more creative attitude on the subject of war and peace than its English counterpart. Among British Friends the quietist atmosphere continued undisturbed.

In Great Britain as well as in those American colonies where Quakers were not in control the negative aspects of the peace testimony for long remained uppermost in the minds of eighteenth-century Friends. Members of the Society who attended muster or hired substitutes or paid their militia fines, or who were connected either as owners or crew with vessels armed to resist attack, were systematically dealt with by their meetings. If unwilling to express regret at their conduct and change their ways, they were finally disowned. In general, "there was an increasing tendency for Friends to believe that, provided they complied . . . in a legalistic sense, they were doing sufficient and that it was not necessary to see that they were complying . . . in spirit" (Richard E. Stagg).

Most trouble was experienced in keeping members of meetings in coastal areas from deviating from the rules. This was as true of Rhode Island or Nantucket as of Yorkshire or Cornwall, despite the fact that on each side of the Atlantic the respective Yearly Meetings passed minutes deploring what on one occasion was described as "a flagrant and lamentable departure from our peaceable principle." With their living depending on the sea Quaker mariners and shipowners found it difficult to adhere exactly to a pacifist witness and boycott all vessels carrying armaments. Even though their involvement in the business of war was not the result of any legal compulsion, it was indeed harder for them than for those called up for the militia, whose livelihood was not jeopardized by refusal to serve. We may note, however, that although, by the end of the eighteenth century at any rate, a few Quaker shipowners in Britain seem to have resorted to the dubious expedient of installing dummy wooden guns on their vessels to frighten away attackers, such "Quaker guns", as they were called, were used almost exclusively by non-Quakers, who wished in this way to avoid costly armaments.

A new problem arose with the appearance of Quaker industrialists. In the eighteenth century (as in other periods) the manufacture of armaments was a profitable affair. The Darbys, a Quaker family whose iron foundry at Coalbrookdale helped to pioneer the Industrial Revolution in Britain, preferred loyalty to their Society's principles over commercial profit and refused to make cannon. Quaker businessmen, however, were not always so scrupulous. Their delinquency was sometimes detected and dealt with sternly by the meeting: at other times it seems either to have been passed over in silence or to have remained undiscovered.

Stringency in this respect appears to have increased in the second half of the eighteenth century. Greater sensitivity was now being displayed, too, in regard to war taxes. The traditional views of the Society that Friends should refuse payment only when the money was in lieu of some war service persisted for a long time. Writing in 1756 to an American Quakei, Dr. John Fothergill formulated this position as follows: "Friends have ever refused to be actively concerned in immediate military services and appointments and have scrupled to pay taxes directly for this end." But in the last decade of the century during Britain's war against revolutionary France many Friends refused to pay special war taxes and were supported in this by London Yearly Meeting, even though it does not appear to have issued any overall ruling in the matter. All this reflected a slowly growing awareness on the part of Friends of the wider implications of their peace testimony.

We must now centre our attention on the American scene in order to trace the emergence there around mid-century of a radical pacifist witness among one section of the membership of Philadelphia Yearly Meeting. (This meeting included not only Friends living in Pennsylvania but those in adjacent New Jersey as well.) The American colonies had shared in the long years of peace promoted by Walpole's government: with the outbreak of war in 1739 British North America joined in the fighting along with the mother country. The so-called War of Jenkins' Ear soon merged into the wider War of Austrian Succession, which was ended only in 1748. The commencement of hostilities brought demands for aid from the Deputy Governor of Pennsylvania representing the proprietors. (The Penn family indeed were no longer Quakers.) He now asked the provincial assembly to set up a militia to include all able-bodied men who were not conscientiously opposed to bearing arms and to provide funds for placing the province's defences on a war footing. The Quaker dominated assembly reacted to this request and to subsequent demands of a similar character as it had done on earlier occasions. First entering upon an acrimonious debate with the Deputy-Governor, it ended by acceding at least to his plea for money. The time-worn formulae — "for the king's use," "a tribute to Caesar" — came in handy once again. In 1745, when the war was under way, the assemblymen directed the sum then granted be used "in the purchase of bread, beef, pork, flour, wheat or other grain." "I shall take the money," commented the Deputy-Governor, "for I understand very well their meaning; *other grain,* is gunpowder."

Even if there is more malice than truth in this remark, clearly a certain ambiguity existed in the attitude of the assembly's Quaker majority. Not only critics like Benjamin Franklin who shared neither the Quakers' religion nor their pacifism and strove during the war to establish a voluntary defense force in the province, felt this to be so. There was an increasing number within the Society of Friends itself, who considered the viewpoint represented by the Quaker politicians no longer adequate to the demands of the time. On the one hand, some nonpacifist Quakers like James Logan urged the Society, since it could not consistently approve measures of self-defence, to imitate the behaviour of Friends in Great Britain (whose abstention from political activity, however resulted from their legal disabilities) and advise its pacifist members henceforward to refrain from holding public office "above those of the respective parishes where they live." We find, on the other hand, the same conclusions being reached from around mid-century by a group of Quakers within Pennsylvania Yearly Meeting concerned to restore the purity of their Society's peace testimony. These peace radicals were eventually to bring about an almost complete retreat from public life.

The radical group drew its main strength from the rural meetings, but it found some support in Philadelphia, too, Its leaders included above all John Woolman, the New Jersey tailor, whose *Journal* ranks among the classic religious autobiographies, and the French born Anthony Benezet, like Woolman an ardent crusader on behalf of all oppressed and suffering creatures. Woolman in particular drew Friends' attention to the connection between wealth and war. "Wealth", he wrote, "is attended with power, by which bargains and proceedings contrary to universal righteousness are supported; and here oppression, carried on with worldly policy and order, clothes itself with the name of justice, and becomes like a seed of discord in the soul: and as this spirit which wanders from the pure habitation prevails, so the seed of war swells and sprouts and grows and becomes strong till much fruit are ripened. Then cometh the harvest..." Worldly possessions must be regaded as a trust and war as a punishment from God for abusing this trust. Woolman and his associates called upon the well-to-do Quakers of Philadelphia to take stock of their position and see if their wealth as well as their involvement in politics did not contain the seeds of violence. If this were so — and the radicals believed it was — then Friends must abandon political life and prepare their minds for the sacrifice of prosperity, should this too become necessary. Otherwise the Society, if it continued to be politically active, would eventually lose the reality, if not yet "the name of a peaceable people," for its pacifist principles would be contradicted by its practical policies.

The outbreak of frontier fighting in the summer of 1755 proved to be the opening phase of a French and Indian War, which developed in the following year into a struggle between France and England on a global scale. Usually known as the Seven Years' War, the conflict came to an end only in 1763. The commencement of hostilities caused great tension in Pennsylvania. The inhabitants of the frontier areas, almost all non-Quakers, demanded defensive measures against the Indian attacks which were inspired by the French, and the home authorities, too, insisted the province take its share in imperial defense. In November the Quaker assemblymen who still controlled the house, following their traditional pattern of behaviour, agreed to an appropriation of sixty thousand pounds "for the king's use"; in addition, they sanctioned the setting up of a voluntary militia. Only seven Quaker deputies voted against the grant of money and as few as four voted against the militia bill. The radicals' hour had arrived.

In the following month they issued an open letter to their fellow members which they entitled "An Epistle of Tender Love and Caution to Friends in Pennsylvania." Woolman was chiefly responsible for drawing it up. The epistle advocated startling changes in the stand hitherto taken by Pennsylvania Quakers. Implicitly it challenged their involvement in politics: indeed, if it did not call in doubt the very principles on which the "holy experiment" was based, at least it denied the validity of their application in the existing situation. Moreover, the document called explicitly on Friends to undertake a campaign of civil disobedience by refusing to pay taxes in time of war. This represented a complete reversal not only of the practice of Pennsylvania Friends but of the Society's teaching from the days of George Fox on. While not attempting in principle to overthrow the accepted view which approved payment of taxes "in the mixture", the epistle argued that, as things then stood, taxation was "so mixed" with the carrying on of war that a consistent Friend would have no alternative but to refuse payment altogether — even if this meant passive resistance to the laws of a Quaker controlled legislature. The penalties of breaking the law must be endured patiently: it was preferable to suffer material loss so long as Truth prevailed.

In their campaign to "depoliticize" their Society the Pennsylvania radicals found unexpected allies among the leaders of London Yearly Meeting. True, many of these "English Friends were less conscientious and pacifistic than their American Brethren" of the Woolman kind (Jack D. Marietta). And however much some country Friends in England might sympathize with the American radicals' stand, the Quaker establishment in London was totally opposed to tax resistance of this sort. But it was also less politically inclined than the Quaker establishment in Philadelphia. It saw more clearly than the latter that, at least for the time being, a religious body professing pacifist principles would only lose respect if it continued its close link to an administration engaged in carrying on war. London Yearly Meeting, therefore, began to put pressure on its Philadelphia counterpart so as to induce a temporary withdrawal of members from the provincial assembly. Faced by opposition from two sides those Quaker assemblymen who remained closest to the Society — six in number — resigned their seats in June 1756.

52

Even after the Quaker "politiques" had departed, the Quaker "politicians" (to use Richard Bauman's distinction) remained and their so-called "Quaker Party" continued in control of the assembly for many years to come. None were expelled from the Society, unless for speaking out publicly against the peace testimony which they no longer shared: some of them may still have preserved a personal objection to bearing arms derived from their Quaker background. However, when this group now claimed in extenuation of their conduct that, since they were "not active in the immediate application of the sums granted," they could not be held to have "wounded the testimony of Friends" (as was argued, for instance, in 1760), their sentiments found little response among their fellow members. While only a minority followed the radicals and became tax objectors, consistent Quakers mostly withdrew now from public office: in 1758, as a result of the campaign of Woolman and his friends, Philadelphia Yearly Meeting had advised strongly against acceptance of even the lower magistracy. And subsequently it reenacted this decision every few years.

The process of withdrawal from politics and renewal of the peace testimony, which the mid-century Quaker radicals had initiated, was carried to completion as a consequence of Friends' experiences during the American Revolution. American Friends opposed the war which broke out between colonists and mother country in 1775 on two counts. In the first place, as pacifists they could not participate of course in the fighting — on either side. But a second, and complicating, factor existed in their war resistance. Like the Mennonites, Quakers, too, regarded loyalty to the powers that be as a religious duty which they must uphold even at the cost of suffering. Suspicion that Quaker and "Tory" were interchangeable terms became widespread, especially in regard to the rich Quaker merchants of Philadelphia who, ironically, "far from being Tories in the usual sense, had stood for years as outspoken exponents of the Whig ideals of liberty and property" (Frederick B. Tolles). If a few Tory sympathizers were to be found among members of the Society — as among other denominations — the overwhelming majority of Quakers strove to uphold a position of nonviolent neutrality during the years of conflict. As one of them put it: "It was impossible for a true Quaker to be either Whig or Tory, for they implied opposite parties, and both believed in war, but Friends did not."

Only a few Friends, then, espoused the British cause. A larger group — but still small when compared with the whole Society in America — gave militant support to the Revolution: after failing to gain even the tacit approval of the Society for those who joined the Revolutionary army, these members seceded, however, and formed their own meeting of Free Quakers. This did not succeed in recruiting many adherents and eventually disappeared.

The Quaker discipline ensured that Friends, if they desired to remain members in good standing, neither fought themselves nor gave support to the war effort of either contestant. All the evidence indicates that, with only a few exceptions, the American Society wholeheartedly backed this position of nonbelligerency. It had been purified by the efforts of the preceding generation of reformers, and even Philadelphia grandees now "consciously imitated seventeenth-century Friends" in their willingness to suffer material loss and to endure persecution for their faith (Marietta).

The pattern of conscientious objection during the American Revolution remained the same as in earlier periods in respect to military service. Quakers were precluded, too, from assisting either of the conflicting armies with their labour: farmers, for instance, who voluntarily handed over their horses and carts for employment by the military became liable to disciplinary action by their local meeting. The tax issue continued to cause much heart searching among Friends. During the three decades preceding the outbreak of the Revolutionary War the radical position had gained ground, though it never became a universally accepted position within the Society. During the war the question — to pay or not to pay? — was debated vigorously. Little doubt now existed that most of the taxes imposed by the Revolutionary authorities, though in theory "mixed", were destined to be used chiefly for military purposes. Many Friends, therefore, would not pay them. And there were those who went even further and advocated a complete tax boycott. A New England Quaker reports of his area: "Some Friends refuse all taxes, even those for civil uses as well as those clear for war and others that are mixed." There were further war problems too, which exercised the minds of Friends. When the American authorities imposed an oath of loyalty to the new régime, the Society forbade its members to take the Test, even though the government recognized Quakers' long standing objection to judicial oaths and were ready to agree to the substitutin of a mere affirmation. In this instance, as in the case of the minority of Friends refusing to accept the paper money issued by the Revolutionary government (which hoped to finance the war by this means), the primary motive stemmed from the Quakers' unwillingness to switch loyalty at the behest of an insurgent power. But their refusal was connected, too, with their witness for peace. Acquiescence in demands of this kind seemed to constitute an overt recognition of the validity of the war method for solving human disputes.

The Revolutionary authorities reacted quickly — and sharply — to the Quaker position. Conscientious objectors were imprisoned, occasionally for as long as two years. Active opponents of the war were sometimes roughly handled. In 1777 a group of wealthy Philadelphia Friends, falsely accused of treason, were deported to Virginia. But members of the Society suffered most heavily as a result of the financial penalties for resistance to wartime decrees. Their goods were distrained and their property requisitioned to the value of over one hundred thousand pounds. This seemed to confirm Woolman's message: worldly possessions and Quaker peacableness had now proved incompatible in fact as well as in theory.

The Society of Friends emerged from the years of war a rather different body from the one it had been on the eve of the Revolution. The "politicians" had disappeared from its midst. Most of them had actively thrown in their lot with the new régime; the few genuine Tories had departed for Canada along with other Empire Loyalists. True, in the postwar years Quakers, like Mennonites, soon began to feel themselves to be "essentially good Americans" (Stanley V. James), while differing from the overwhelming majority of their fellow citizens, among other matters, on the question of war. It is true, too, that, once the war was over, the new administration from its side began to look with increasing favour on the sect it had once regarded with deep suspicion as a clique of crypto-Tories. We now find President Washington telling a leading Quaker who had been expounding his Society's peace principles: "I honour your sentiments; there is more in them than mankind have generally considered." But the days were gone when the Society of Friends represented a significant factor on the American political scene. Only very slowly did Friends once again enter politics, and they did so now as individuals in no way representative of their brethren. The American Revolution did not drive the Society into the wilderness as it did almost literally in the case of the German speaking peace sects. Although urban Quakers and cultivated Quakers who contributed to the cultural life of their nation continued to exist alongside the country Quakers of the rural meetings, in the new United States the Society of Friends existed as it were in "a garden enclosed". The radical spirit, having regenerated the Quaker witness for peace, had come to rest. What appeared at the beginning as the breath of renewal, was transformed at last into the conventional stance of the Society.

By the end of the eighteenth century, however, a new era was again dawning in the history of the Quaker peace testimony, as in the life of the Society as a whole. Religious quietism was retreating in the English branch before the advance of the evangelical movement, and on both sides of the Atlantic the humanitarian sentiment, which would typify Friends' outlook on life in the nineteenth and twentieth centuries, was already extending its influence on the Quaker ethos. Their first essay in organizing relief for the civilian victims of war came at the outset of the American Revolution when they sent supplies into beleaguered Boston which was besieged in succession by British and American armies. The spread of the continental variety of egalitarian democracy from the time of the French Revolution on, which acted so devastatingly on the European Mennonites' faith in nonresistance, presented fewer problems for American and English Quakers. They had been themselves pioneers in developing the British tradition of liberty: their peace witness proved more adaptable to the new currents of thought. And, moreover, the militaristic nationalism which expanded rapidly on the European continent, though not entirely absent in English speaking countries, proved less threatening to the Quaker peace testimony than to the Mennonite tradition of nonresistance.

(c)   *The Nineteenth Century*

American Quakers remained politically inactive much longer than their co-religionists in England, where members of the Society of Friends began to enter parliament soon after the final removal of political restrictions on non-Anglicans in 1829. This aloofness from politics on the part of Quakers in the United States was reflected in respect of the peace testimony in their general unwillingness — aside from a few individal Friends untypical of the Society as a whole — to collaborate with the new peace societies which sprang up on both sides of the Atlantic at the end of the Napoleonic Wars. This nonsectarian pacifism forms the subject of the next chapter. Here we need only consider briefly the attitude which American and British Friends respectively adopted towards it.

For most American Friends of this period the activities of the peace societies, however laudable their ultimate aim of achieving international peace might be, appeared to be too intimately bound up with the affairs of the world to deserve anything more than lukewarm approval. "It is safer," declared a Quaker periodical published in Philadelphia, "that we keep much to ourselves, and not act as a body in reference to this important testimony, lest by joining with others we should unawares be led into a compromise or evasion of any of its requisitions." When a radical wing of the American peace movement emerged in the late 1830's, the lukewarmness which official Quakerism had shown towards the moderate peace men, turned into downright hostility. The handful of Friends who supported the radicals were frowned upon and in some places subjected to disciplinary action by local meetings. From their side the leaders of the peace movement of whatever complexion, while expressing their admiration of the Society's steadfast witness for peace and drawing upon it when expounding their principles to the public, also expressed their surprise and disappointment at the lack of cooperation they met with from Friends as a whole. While this uncooperativeness stemmed either from fear that the less uncompromising position of the peace moderates might lead eventually to a watering down of the Quaker peace testimony or from the radicals' extremism, its basic cause lay in American Friends' general outlook on public affairs. They saw their political role now as a purely passive one. Most members voted at elections, but few went further than this.

The position of British Friends was quite different. Having been excluded by *force majeure* from playing an active part in politics — unlike the American Society which, after tasting the fruits of power, had carried out a voluntary withdrawal from a conviction of its unchristian character — they did not shun participation in political life when its possibility opened up for them. And among the most effective public areas in which they could bring their influence to bear in favour of Quaker principles was the organized peace movement. Indeed the English movement was in large part a Quaker creation, and Quakers remained its devoted adherents. The Victorian political leader, Richard Cobden, rightly called Friends "the soul of the peace movement" in Britain. The original idea of setting up a Peace Society took shape in the London home of a Quaker philanthropist and businessman in 1814, and after its formal inauguration two years later Quakers continued to be conspicuous both on the executive and among the membership at large. In fact, "Quakers were a majority among subscribers to the Peace Society" (Eric W. Sager).

The drive towards social action brought by the evangelical movement which deeply influenced Quakerism from around the outset of the nineteenth century, combined with the optimistic humanitarian spirit inherited from the eighteenth-century Enlightenment, led Friends on both sides of the Atlantic to become active moral reformers. Slavery, war, drink, crime and other problems of society now engaged Quakers' collective attention to an extent not visible before. In Britain they broke free from their narrow sectarian enclosure earlier than in the United States and joined with the reform minded of the other Protestant denominations to press for public action in matters of common concern.

In regard to war the older, somewhat negative stance was transformed into a more positive testimony which stressed the need to eliminate war as a method of settling international disputes more than the obligation to avoid complicity in the military machine. Penn was the model here rather than Fox. Quaker pacifism, it is true, was still based on the New Testament precepts of peace, and on the Sermon on the Mount in particular, and it was still basically moral rather than utilitarian in outlook. But, at least in so far as the British Society was concerned, its witness did not differ on any essential point from that of pacifists from other Christian churches.

This can be seen in the work for peace of two English Quakers, Jonathan Dymond who died prematurely in 1828 aged only 31, and John Bright whose long and active career ended in 1889. Dymond became well known outside the Society of Friends only after his death when his exposition of Quaker pacifism, published in several different versions, soon grew to be one of the most popular works distributed by the pre-1914 peace movement. "Dymond on peace" was read by many thousands who had no other contact with Quakerism. For Dymond urged his case in simple and straightforward language without using an overabundance of Biblical citations with which earlier pacifist apologists had usually burdened their pages. And he argued persuasively that in practice all international disputes could be resolved without resorting to arms. Like other contemporary peace advocates, he saw arbitration as the panacea for eliminating war. "If nations fought only when they could not be at peace, there would be very little fighting in the world," he wrote. A just war of defense, though conceivable in theory, was impossible in practice: Dymond saw the origins of war in the pursuit of economic self-interest and national glory as well as in an oversensitive national pride. In the light of human reason, therefore, and not merely according to the precepts of religion, all war stood condemned.

The rational case against war, the optimistic faith that war might be eliminated by human effort which was typical of all peace advocates in the nineteenth century, had an even more effective protagonist in the person of John Bright. For Bright was a successful politician, while Dymond remained the secluded man of letters. Bright, though he was a devoted member of the Society of Friends, never urged pacifism as a national policy. He was certainly not a nonresistant. Whether privately he shared the Quaker version of pacifism to the full is a disputable question (I incline myself to think he did). But when the cartoonists depicted Bright in Quaker garb, inaccurately since in fact he had discarded it early in his political career, their feeling was right nevertheless. There is something essentially Quakerly about Bright's whole political outlook — nineteenth-century British Quakerly, that is, for he probably would not have pleased either George Fox or John Woolman too much.

Bright condemned war on pragmatic grounds: "he always argued the question on a blue-book basis" (Margaret E. Hirst). He pointed to material damage inflicted, to economic and political progress blocked, to morality threatened as a result of armed conflict. Like Dymond and other contemporary peace advocates, he detected the roots of war in national ambition and greed: lik them, too, he underestimated the force of ideological factors as then displayed in the armed struggles of oppressed nationalities of Europe like the Italians or Hungarians. In Bright's view, an alternative to war almost always existed, provided the imperialistic expansionism of the ruling classes in each country were overcome. This made resort to arms unnecessary and therefore unjustifiable. True, there were a few exceptions to this rule: Bright thought Lincoln's administration, for instance, was right in fighting against the attempt at secession by the South. But such occasions resulted from a domestic breakdown of order rather than from a conflict between states. Though he may have differed from most of his fellow Quakers in defining police action more broadly than they did, Bright was at one with his Society in advocating the total abolition of war as an instrument of national policy.

Time and again British Friends lined up with Bright and his colleagues of the parliamentary "peace party" in opposing the various colonial campaigns in which Great Britain engaged during Victoria's reign. This alliance emerged most visibly during the Crimean War when Tsarist Russia became the enemy. (Bright and Cobden, who were both vigorous antagonists of the Russophobia that repeatedly swept nineteenth-century England, in the process sometimes did injustice to the claims of peoples like the Poles who suffered under Tsardom's yoke.) Early in 1854, as war appeared imminent, London Friends decided to send a three-man delegation to the Tsar to urge the necessity of maintaining peace. The delegates succeeded in obtaining an interview with Nicholas I, during which they were able to explain the basis of the Quaker peace testimony. Though the Tsar was sympathetic — the delegates had not tried to discuss responsibility for the existing conflict — events took their course and war broke out soon after. Though unsuccessful, the delegation marked the beginning of collective Quaker efforts at what may be termed private diplomacy, a form of peace action which the Society was to develop more intensively in the next century. After hostilities with Russia had commenced Quakers carried through "the most successful pacifist propaganda effort of the Crimean War" (Stephen Frick): the mass distribution of a leaflet, of which many thousands of copies were printed, entitled *A Christian Appeal from the Society of Friends to Their Fellow-Countrymen on the Present War*. "That which is morally or religiously wrong cannot be politically right", was the main thought it attempted to impress on the public.

From the very beginning the Quaker Joseph Sturge waged a lively and vigorous campaign against the war, ably supported by the staunchly pacifist, though non-Quaker secretary of the Peace Society, Henry Richard, in the *Herald of Peace* and by internationalists like Bright and Cobden (efforts which Frick has recently studied in detail). Nevertheless, as Gavin B. Henderson wrote, "the setback that peace ideas had received" as a result of the war was a serious one.

At the same time as British Quakers were imparting to their peace testimony a more distinctly political form, while keeping it firmly anchored on a religious foundation, they began, too, to explore other ways of giving it positive expression. One of these was the relief of noncombatant sufferers from war action: Friends could thereby perform a task of mercy and, in addition, prove that their objection to war went beyond a mere refusal to fight. The organization of war relief combined both their humanitarian and their antimilitarist impulses in a practical shape. During the nineteenth century Quaker relief included work among Greek refugees in the early twenties, in Finland in the late fifties, in France after the Franco-Prussian War of 1870, and in the late seventies in Bulgaria.

Conscientious objection to military service, which had earlier occupied a central place in Friends' witness for peace and would do so again during the global wars of the twentieth century, in the course of the nineteenth century ceased for a time to possess immediate relevance, except in respect to the few small Quaker meetings on the European continent. In France and Germany these disappeared altogether under the burden of universal military service. In Britain a compulsory militia was abandoned in 1860: this for the time being brought to an end the long series of "sufferings" — imprisonment and distraint of property — endured by Friends on account of their refusal to bear arms. In the United States the militia system had become completely moribund by mid-century: it was generally regarded by this date as an irksome anachronism. Compulsion to serve was no longer enforced, and penalties for refusal therefore ceased, too.

Conscription returned, though, after the outbreak of war between Northern and Southern states in 1861. The next four years proved a period of great trial for Friends — as indeed for all pacifists in the now divided country. The guiding principle behind the Quaker peace testimony, to quote from a statement issued early in the war by Baltimore Yearly Meeting, was "love, universal love — love to God, and love to all men." It had led Friends not merely to resist war but in due course to emancipate their slaves rather than keep fellow men in subjection. True, on the issue of slavery they remained gradualists rather than outright abolitionists. Yet they were bound to feel keenly the dilemma posed by a war which was being waged, at any rate ostensibly, for the liberation of the oppressed. How, on one hand, could they refuse to support the war effort of Lincoln's Unionist administration without betraying their long struggle to free the American Blacks? But how, on the other, could they fight on behalf of what most of them considered a righteous cause without turning their backs on their centuries-old witness for nonviolence? The situation appeared to be one in which the traditional answers no longer held good. It was not only the young who felt this, though they felt it most keenly, but often older Friends, too, like the poet John Greenleaf Whittier for instance, found it difficult to overcome all doubt. As President Lincoln himself expressed it: "In this hard dilemma some [Quakers] have chosen one horn and some the other." There were Friends who strove to achieve a compromise, a kind of nonviolent support for the Unionist cause — by looking after the wounded, for example, or supplying garments needed for the troops. Others, while not denying the strength of the Unionist position, felt it to be their duty to uphold an uncompromisingly pacifist stand and refrain from any voluntary collaboration with the war effort.

Quakers of military age had perforce to make a well defined choice: to serve or not to serve in the armed forces. (Alternative service under civilian control was not offered at this time.) At the outset of the struggle many young Quakers in the Northern states rushed to join the colours. "Old Quaker women see their sons go, without a tear," reported an eye-witness from a small Pennsylvania town. With these men the antislavery impulse, combined with patriotic zeal, had proved more compelling than the traditional teaching on war of their sect. Those who defected from pacifism now were a minority, but a sizeable minority, "more numerous than one would have expected in a conservative body which made the [peace] testimony an absolutely essential feature of its faith" (Rufus M. Jones). Quaker volunteers came mostly from urban meetings which were on the whole less traditionalist and more subject to the often unconscious pressures of public opinion than country Friends were. Whereas in earlier times bearing arms had resulted inevitably in disownment if the offending Friend failed to express contrition for his infraction of the Society's discipline, in the American Civil War this was not always the case. Again it was the urban meetings, where support for the Unionist cause often embraced the elders as well as the young Friends, that deviated most strikingly from the inherited norm of Quaker conduct. Here the fighting Quaker was sometimes accepted as having followed his conscience as truly as his brother who became a conscientious objector. In a much greater number of cases proceedings were at least postponed until after the fighting was over, thus making reconciliation easier between the meeting and its warriors returned now from the war. The latter were usually ready to acknowledge that their active participation had constituted an unwarranted departure from the Quaker path and to ask to be continued in membership. A few refused to do so and left the Society for good.

Lincoln's administration provided for objectors in its conscription laws, though for some time it failed to distinguish explicitly between men whose objections to the draft derived from religious scruples and those who did not wish to serve for some other, less conscientious reason. Both categories had only to pay a commutation fee of $300 in lieu of military service: having done so, they were free to pursue their peace time avocations. Undoubtedly generous in intention, this exemption, however, could not satisfy the strict Quaker conscience which, we have seen, balked at paying money in exchange for doing what it considered right. But as in the case of Quaker combatancy, payment of commutation money which had formerly been regarded by the Society of Friends as an infringement of its discipline was seldom dealt with now as strictly as in the old days. The Quaker periodicals debated the matter at length without being able to reach a generally acceptable position. The situation improved slightly when in 1864 the government allowed genuine pacifists, instead of doing military service, to choose either noncombatant duties under the supervision of the Secretary of War — hospital work and "the care of freedmen" were the two assignments mentioned in the act — or the payment of the same commutation fee as before, which, however, would be used now only to help "sick and wounded soldiers" and not applied to directly military purposes, as had happened earlier. This certainly eased the consciences of those Quaker conscripts who were willing to cooperate and for those meetings — in fact the overwhelming majority — which were ready to acquiesce in this. But it did not help the situation of the absolutist objectors who remained loyal to the traditional pattern of Quaker behaviour in rejecting all conditions attached to exemption. Some of these men got off comparatively lightly, merely suffering distraint on their property. Others, however, were forcibly inducted into the army and had to endure various tribulations there before being released as a result of Friends' intervention on their behalf with the President and Secretary of War, both of whom proved on the whole sympathetic. The military authorities were probably not displeased to see their Quakers go.*

The position of the conscientious objector in the Confederate States was paradoxically both easier and more difficult than that of his northern brother. He did not have to choose between two Quaker testimonies: peace and antislavery. For his government was waging war to maintain the "peculiar institution". He did not, therefore, face the agonizing dilemma of young Quakers in the North, for whom often a decision either way appeared as a betrayal of the principles of their faith. There were indeed few from among the Southern Quaker meetings who chose to fight. These meetings were anyhow small in size: they were situated mainly in the state of North Carolina. On the other hand, the lot of the Southern objector was frequently harder than in the North: the conscription laws to which he was subject were harsher and the Confederate administration less sympathetic. The White community as a whole proved less understanding than on the Unionist side where familiarity with Quaker ways was more widespread.

The Confederate government, as a result of the lobbying carried on by Quakers as well as by the Mennonites and Brethren, eventually agreed to exempt religious objectors on condition they paid $500 for this privilege. Even though payment of commutation money, as we know, conflicted with Friends' discipline, in this instance "the Yearly Meeting . . . allowed its members to avail themselves of the exemption . . . if they could conscientiously do so" (Edward Needles Wright). A small number refused to take this way out and, after induction into the army, suffered severe hardships, including the application of torture in some cases. This also was the lot of two other groups of Quaker objectors — members who had joined the Society after passing of the conscription act and were therefore not covered by its provisions, and attenders at Quaker meetings who shared the Society's views on war but had not actually joined it.

On both sides of the battle line Quakers had succeeded in maintaining their traditional testimony against war. There had been some wavering and defection, mostly in the North. But the Society as a whole stood firm. We can observe, however, some relaxation of the formerly rigid discipline. A more tolerant attitude begins to appear, if still rather diffidently: we have seen that those who followed conscience in respect to their wartime activity, even where this did not coincide with the regulations of the Society, were not always faced now with either having to do penance or leaving altogether.

The American Civil War proved to be the only nineteenth-century conflict in which large numbers of Friends were personally involved. On its close an era of peace ensued for the United States. The attention of American Quakers was diverted to other problems: for some time ahead war ceased to figure as a major concern of the Society of Friends. The Society itself was undergoing important changes from within. Earlier in the century the tide of evangelicalism had engulfed first British Quakerism and then the American Society where it caused a deep cleavage among Friends. In 1827 the first of several "separations" occurred which have not yet been entirely overcome. Internal division, however, was balanced to some extent by territorial expansion: Quakers formed one of the elements making up the great movement of the American people into the sparsely inhabited territories of the West. New meetings sprang up in these areas; fresh recruits were drawn into membership, sometimes without fully absorbing the old Quaker ethos, including the peace testimony. These new Friends in many cases abandoned the traditional way of Quaker worship and chose pastors to guide their religious life, like all their Protestant neighbours did. Some Western meetings succumbed to the wave of fundamentalist preaching which swept this part of the country in the latter decades of the nineteenth century: they soon came to regard Eastern Quakerism, and even some of their pastoral brethren, as excessively liberal. And one of the manifestations of this liberalism seemed to them to be pacifism, which Quaker fundamentalists eventually discarded altogether. Most of their young men were to serve in the armed forces during the two world wars of the present century.

Although it is true the problem of peace did not again become a primary concern of American Friends of the Quaker mainstream until around the end of the nineteenth century, steps began to be taken much earlier to reactivate the peace testimony. In 1867 the evangelical branch (who were known as Orthodox) set up a Peace Association of Friends in America. This body distributed peace literature, including a monthly journal, and organized public meetings and lectures on peace as well. It did not restrict its publications to works by Quaker authors, reprinting the writings of peace advocates of other denominations. A new spirit in respect to peace work began to emerge, especially among younger Friends of the Eastern states: a desire to break out finally from the Quaker enclosure and collaborate with others in the crusade against war and in bringing pressure on governments in the direction of peace. As one of this group most active on behalf of peace remarked: "We must accomplish something with those who determine the destiny of nations." A highly respected Friend held the secretaryship of the American Peace Society from 1892 to 1915: a far cry from the days, not so long before, when Quakers held aloof from the nonsectarian peace movement for fear the purity of their witness against war should be sullied by contact with outsiders. Standing peace committees began to be set up by the various yearly meetings. Quaker periodicals gave increased space to protests against the spread of militarism and ever mounting armaments and to articles in favour of international arbitration, and Friends of different persuasions (apart from the fundamentalists) jointly organized conferences where the political as well as the religious implications of their peace testimony were discussed. Only the economic case against war was neglected: American Friends, when they were not still farmers, belonged mostly to the urban middle class and had little, if any, contact with labour or left-wing radicalism.

On the eve of World War I, therefore, the position on peace of American Friends — or at least of a significant part of the American Society — approximated that of British Friends, except that the latter included a small group of active Christian socialists who strove to convince their fellow members of the dangers of clashing imperialisms and of the struggle of capitalist rivals for markets overseas. The English Society in the course of the nineteenth century had declined seriously in numbers, largely due to the custom of disowning members who had "married out". The decline ceased after the rules were in general made less stringent. In respect to the peace testimony the volunteer system by which Britain filled her peacetime army and navy removed the burden of conscription which weighed ever more heavily on the peoples of the European continent. It was not reimposed until 1916. The fact that in the 1914-18 War about a third of the Friends of military age served in one of the armed forces shows that, after the Quaker discipline had fallen into disuse, the number of those who did not share the Society's pacifism grew. But we also have to remember these fighting Quakers were often drawn from those whose membership tended to be merely nominal.

The Society of Friends — in North America as well as in Great Britain — entered the twentieth century with the fundamental principles of its antimilitarism virtually unchanged since these crystallized around the time of the Stuart Restoration. Its basis remained personal: the individual Quaker's refusal to fight because war conflicted with Christian morality as members of the Society interpreted this. What had changed was the form in which the Quaker peace testimony was embodied. Conscientious objection still remained at its core but during the nineteenth century a process of "politicization" and "socialization" of this testimony had begun. It no longer seemed enough for Quakers simply to refuse to fight. They must join with other men of good will in first seeking to discover the causes of war and violence in the international and social order and then working to remove them. And should war come nevertheless, Friends now saw their task in aiding its victims so far as their resources allowed. The two world wars of the present century did not bring to an end the Quaker search for peace.

---

*[Page 60, line 4] For the attitude of Lincoln and his administration to Quaker conscientious objectors, see Daniel Bassuk, *Abraham Lincoln and the Quakers,* Pendle Hill Pamphlet 273 (Wallingford [Pennsylvania]), 1987, pp. 19-23. And for the standpoint of a young Friend who volunteered for the Union Army and died during service, see Peter H. Curtis, "A Quaker and the Civil War: The Life of James Parnell Jones", *Quaker History* (Haverford, Pennsylvania), vol LXVII, no. 1 (Spring 1978), pp. 35-41.

4. NONSECTARIAN PACIFISM IN THE NINETEENTH CENTURY

(a) *The Moderates*

The first peace societies came into existence in Great Britain and the United States almost simultaneously. The New York Peace Society had been founded by a pious and philanthropic businessman named David Low Dodge in August 1815, while in the following year similar bodies were set up in June in London and in December in Boston, Massachusetts. The London Peace Society resulted from the efforts of a group of concerned individuals, including Quakers as well as members of other Protestant denominations; the Massachusetts Peace Society was the creation of a Unitarian clergyman, Noah Worcester. Whereas hitherto pacifist views had been confined exclusively to members of such sects as the Mennonites or Quakers, apart from a few scattered individuals in other churches who objected to all war, now nonsectarian pacifism found organized expression. That this occurred at this date was not due to chance. The early nineteenth-century peace movement on both sides of the Atlantic formed part of a broader current of humanitarian reform, which affected both Britain and the United States and helped to bring to birth antislavery societies and Sunday Schools as well as Bible societies and associations for penal reform, to cite only some of the most important products of this philanthropic zeal, which stemmed from a vision, shared by the reformers of the two countries, of "making the millennium" (Alexander Tyrrell).

The year 1815 had seen the end of a long and exhausting war: Napoleon's defeat ushered in a prolonged period of international quiet. War weariness and postwar optimism, therefore, provided a suitable atmosphere for a concerted attempt at "the promotion of permanent and universal peace," the avowed aim of all the peace societies of that time.

In addition to sharing the same ultimate goal these societies had much in common in respect to membership, activities, and ideology. They were all predominantly middle class in composition. Ministers of religion, businessmen, and members of the free professions formed their core. Few from the very poor or from the very rich and the highly placed joined their ranks. In the London Peace Society aristocratic names were almost entirely absent from the list of members; we do, however, find persons from the Boston merchant patriciate as well as some prominent state officials in the American Peace Society (a body formed in 1828 from a fusion of the Massachusetts and New York societies). In the United States, while few Episcopalians and no Roman Catholics collaborated in the work of the peace movement, the leading Protestant denominations — Baptists, Congregationalists, Methodists, Presbyterians, Universalists and Unitarians — each contributed their quota of members, even though these churches remained generally unsympathetic, or at best neutral, towards the movement. In Great Britain, on the other hand, individual Anglicans, especially evangelical members of the established church like the antislavery leader, Thomas Clarkson, were prominent in the counsels of the London Peace Society. Quakers, we have seen, played a big role in the British peace movement, while standing aloof for the most part in the United States. Of the dozen or so small American sects which professed pacifist views during the nineteenth century, only the Shakers who practised celibacy as well as communitarianism (men and women living separately within the confines of the community) were at all active in the peace movement. The rest nursed their separation from the world, which included abstention from organized peace activity as a defense against what they considered to be harmful worldly influences.

At first the peace societies were primarily moral tract societies. By means of the printed word they aspired to undermine the hold the war ethos had gained over civilized society. They circulated — often free — innumerable leaflets, pamphlets and books against war, and they produced a succession of journals dedicated to the same purpose, that is, "to show that war is inconsistent with the spirit of Christianity and the true interests of mankind" (as the London Peace Society expressed it). They set up local branches wherever they could find even a few supporters of their cause. In the United States, for instance, some fifty of these local societies had come into existence within a decade and a half from the commencement of the movement. On both continents branch members helped to distribute peace literature; from time to time they organized public meetings where discussion took place on the international issues of the day and the point of view of the peace movement could be heard. In addition, societies on both sides of the Atlantic corresponded with each other and were occasionally able to organize some gesture of international solidarity if tension rose between states. On the whole all this proved uphill work. Numbers remained small. Even the Protestant clergy, whom the founding fathers of the peace movement had hoped to enlist in large numbers for their cause, proved largely indifferent. Sometimes their attitude was one of hostility to it. What, however, seemed most discouraging to these peace pioneers was not the attacks from press or pulpit which occurred from time to time but the lack of interest their propaganda met with from the general public.

The pioneers were in no way extreme in their advocacy of peace. They were all very respectable members of the community — apart from their peculiar opinions on war. They were mostly strict churchgoers, whom religious unorthodoxy shocked as much as it shocked their nonpacifist coreligionists. The moderation with which they pressed their antiwar views would eventually arouse opposition and anger among members of a new generation who sought more radical methods of expressing their pacifist beliefs. All three of the original societies were prepared to admit members who, while wishing to work for a peaceful world, did not entirely exclude the possibility of a justifiable war of defense. However, David Dodge's short-lived society in New York and the London Peace Society both wrote unconditional opposition to all war into their statutes: their founders shared a Quakerlike faith in nonviolence. Among these Dodge went furthest in his rejection of force: his views approximated those of the nonresistant Mennonites, since he refrained from voting at elections lest he should sanction thereby the use of governmental violence in any form. The others, while rejecting both organized war and capital punishment as incompatible with their religion, mostly approved what they considered to be the beneficial aspects of civil government. On the other hand, Noah Worcester, the founder of the Massachusetts Peace Society, never publicly expressed an opinion as to the validity of absolute pacifism (though privately he may have supported this). Whereas the London Peace Society — as well as Dodge's society — insisted that at least its officers should subscribe to the belief "that all war is inconsistent with Christianity," no requirement on this point figured in the rules of the Boston society. Dodge indeed waxed somewhat indignant at "the lax doctrines advocated" by Worcester and his associates and wondered if these were not responsible for declining zeal on the part of some of his own supporters. For what Worcester sought to destroy was "the custom of war": he was not concerned, at any rate in his public activities, with the personal implications of war resistance.

The whole peace movement, the absolute pacifists as well as the conditionalists, urged utilitarian arguments against war in addition to the time-worn moral and religious ones. They denounced its cruelties, its inevitable inhumanity;

they castigated its wastefulness not only in human life but in destroying man's material wellbeing as well; they branded it as the foe of freedom and justice. All of them believed in the possibility of abolishing at least "public war," war between states — and the sooner this was done, the better for mankind. And all of them urged the need to set up institutional means of resolving international disputes without resort to armed conflict. "A confederacy of nations", "a congress of nations", an international "high court of equity", and international arbitration were among the proposals made by the peace societies, and they called, too, for disarmament as an essential prerequisite for a peaceful world. Here they concentrated their efforts not so much on achieving unilateral disarmament at once as on trying to make some progress towards proportional and simultaneous disarmament. Whereas in the United States Worcester and his successor the ex-sea captain, William Ladd, who was the first to hold office as secretary of the American Peace Society, while firmly rejecting military sanctions in support of an international organization, were greatly concerned from the beginning with practical issues, in Britain "it was not until the religious pacifists of 1815 had been reinforced by free-trade internationalists that their programme became thoroughly practical" (A.C.F. Beales). Even the absolute pacifists in this early phase of the movement almost without exception failed to develop a strategy of nonviolent action as an alternative to armed resistance to evil. Along with the conditionalists, they dealt primarily either with the moral aspects of war or with the institutional problems of peacemaking.

The question of defensive war — "so-called," added many pacifists — provided the movement, especially its American branch, with its most controversial issue. (It was not discussed much, however, by the peace societies on the European continent, since these did not include any members who had adopted a fully pacifist position.) Worcester had attempted to avoid the matter altogether. There were more important things to do for peace, he thought, than to debate an abstract principle. Some of the absolute pacifists, too, thought much as he did: if one banished all but defensive wars from the international scene, they argued, there would be little need to worry. A truly defensive war, however possible in theory, was next to impossible in reality. They experienced no hesitation, therefore, in joining hands with those peace advocates who refused to give up the idea of national self-defense as a last resort in case of external aggression. There were many on both sides who pleaded for tolerance: the kindly William Ladd was one of them, even though he made no secret of his own personal allegiance to "the high ground" of complete pacifism. Let each member feel free to adopt the theoretical position dictated by his conscience so that all might collaborate harmoniously on the practical issues at hand. Ladd never tired of repeating this message to the American Peace Society as, during the 1830's, tempers rose in the course of prolonged debate, debate which was sometimes decidedly acrimonious and which he was unable to stop however hard he tried to do so.

The younger men indeed would not be halted. To them Ladd's position smacked overmuch of compromise. There was something wrong, they declared, with a peace society that welcomed into its ranks both the supporters of war, provided these agreed to oppose only those conflicts they designated as offensive, and war's opponents. What the younger and more radically inclined men now sought from all members was a kind of "teetotal" pledge. Peace societies should be composed solely of total abstainers from war, just as temperance societies were composed only of total abstainers from alcoholic beverages. "War is not the means for the redress of any of our grievances", wrote a young Unitarian pastor, Samuel J. May, who also urged the resurgent nationalities of Europe to adopt a "more excellent way of overcoming evil" and oppression than by arms. Others raised the case of the American Revolution, a sensitive issue with the community at large and one which the official peace men had studiously avoided for fear any questioning of the Revolutionary cause might bring the peace movement into disrepute. Now some pacifists publicly declared the Revolutionaries, while right in resisting the tyranny exercised by the British government, had been mistaken in their methods of carrying on the struggle. In fact, only nonviolent resistance was a fitting response to injustice on the part of those who believed in the teaching of Jesus. Nonpacifist members of the American Peace Society, on the other hand, answered this challenge by contesting the very basis of Christian pacifism. "What is there," one of them asked, "in Christianity to discountenance . . . a defensive war, any more than there is to prohibit the killing of a mad bull or a hungry wolf?"

In 1837 the absolute pacifists succeeded in persuading the Society at its annual meeting to approve a resolution which wrote pacifism into its constitution on the model of the London Peace Society. However, this measure, though intended as a concession which would help to assuage the discontent of the radicals, did not placate them in fact. For in the following year they seceded and set up in Boston their own Non-Resistance Society, which then proceeded to adopt a quasi-anarchist position on the question of civil government. (The New England nonresistants will be discussed in more detail in the next section of this chapter.) Though the American Peace Society's constitution remained as amended for another eight years, little was changed in reality. Nonpacifist members continued active in it alongside those who stood on "the high ground" of complete pacifism. The latter actually emerged weaker from the whole affair as a result of the radicals' defection. Ladd, who died in 1841, was succeeded as secretary of the Society by a man whose opinions on peace were of the most conservative order and whose main desire was to rid the Society of the taint of "ultraism."

The American Peace Society opposed the war with Mexico, which broke out in 1846 — as did large sections of New England society that were unconnected with the peace movement. The same year saw a second schism within the Society. Many of the remaining absolutists now left its ranks in protest against still further watering down of its testimony for peace. When the Civil War came a decade and a half later, the Society as a whole as well as almost all its members gave enthusiastic support to the military effort of the Northern side — on the grounds that the struggle was not really war but justifiable police action.

The leader of the pacifist revolt in 1846 had been an erudite blacksmith, Elihu Burritt, a man of humble origin, self-made, self-taught, who succeeded none the less in mastering scores of foreign languages. Burritt was a universal reformer whose zeal extended to half a dozen causes, among which the cause of peace took a central place. It was Burritt who described the conservatives who now dominated the American Peace Society as "peace advocates of defensive wars." Though Burritt was no extremist — he approved of the noninjurious aspects of civil government, for instance — he felt it useless to continue to collaborate with the peace conservatives. Therefore, later in the same year at the outset of a prolonged visit across the Atlantic he decided to set up a new peace association which he called the League of Universal Brotherhood. At its centre stood a pledge of unconditional war resistance. "We had conceived", wrote Burritt later, "that in travelling from village to village through England, we might find many by the wayside and fireside, especially among the poorer classes, who would be willing to subscribe their names to the pledge and principles of such an organization." Burritt gathered the first signatures from the villagers whom he met while staying at Pershore in Worcestershire. Farmers and artisans proved to be the backbone of the organization, though Burritt succeeded in enlisting middle class support as well. Recruits to the League pledged themselves to refuse military service and withdraw cooperation from all forms of war activity. They promised, too, to work for friendship between the nations and to regard peoples of all races as their brothers and sisters.

There should have been no doubt, therefore, where the League stood in regard to defensive wars. Yet its actual position was, we find, not quite so clearcut as the "teetotal peace pledge" would seem to indicate. Burritt of course never wavered in his opposition to all war. But this was scarcely the case with the rank and file. For one thing, it is far from certain if all signatories realized the full impact of what they had agreed to. From among the tens of thousands many were undoubtedly mere paper signatures. It did not entail much effort simply to sign one's name. Burritt and his nearest associates worked indefatigably for the cause. The same could not be said, however, for the mass of his peace pledgers. In many cases they could not be relied on if war came (a lesson that Britain's Peace Pledge Union of the 1930's, which adopted a similar pledge as the basis of membership, discovered in 1939). Again, while Burritt was not particularly successful in obtaining signatures on the European continent, he did manage to get some in France, Germany, and the Netherlands. Is it likely that the signatories in these conscriptionist countries were really committing themselves to the full pacifist position, anyhow as a man like Burritt understood this? Indeed the implications of signing were not entirely clear. Must one be a complete nonresistant ready to renounce physical force even in self-defence before he signed? Did one pledge oneself to oppose capital punishment as well as war or was this a matter for each individual to decide according to his conscience? In the United States, where Burritt's idea in fact made less progress than in Britain, it was suspected many of the signatures resulted more from protest against the policy of "Manifest Destiny" which had recently embroiled the country in aggressive war than from adherence to the "high ground" on which Burritt himself stood. For in his native America at least Burritt was ready to accept as associate members persons unable conscientiously to take a pledge of unconditional war resistance.

The League's activities died away during the 1850's. In the United States the rising sectional strife which was to lead to civil war early in the next decade proved unfavourable to a movement like Burritt's. In Great Britain it was the Crimean War that dealt the League a blow from which it failed to recover. And on the European continent, we have seen, it never really got off the ground at all. Burritt's League, though, occupies an important place in the development of pacifism for all its defects in organization and tactics. In the first place it was the first peace society to be set up on an avowed international basis (even if it was largely Anglo-American in its actual composition). Secondly the League broke free from the middle class respectability of the older peace societies and for a brief while succeeded in winning a broader social base for its uncompromisingly antiwar programme than these had been able to do.

With the disappearance of the League of Universal Brotherhood the moderate pacifists in the United States ceased to possess a rallying point for their activities. In Britain, on the other hand, the London Peace Society, whose secretary throughout most of the second half of the nineteenth century was a devoted Christian pacifist, continued to provide an umbrella for the absolutists as well as the conditionalists. In this period several new peace societies emerged here: their chief concern was with problems of international organization, however, and they did not take a stand *vis-à-vis* the question of conscientious objection.

Across the Atlantic the Civil War dealt all sections of the peace movement a heavy blow. It took the American Peace Society many years to recover the confidence of a public, which, despite its own support of war, was shocked at the spectacle of peace people crying loudly for battle; and in fact the Society was never to regain the vigour of earlier days. For many decades after the conflict was over the whole peace movement remained in a state of decline. From the 1890's, however, we see the emergence of a crop of new peace societies, sometimes with fairly large membership. None of these raised the pacifist issue in their discussions, and some of them were even more conservative in outlook than the American Peace Society had ever been. Like their European counterparts they were occupied chiefly with arbitration, international law, and world government. Far from wishing any thoroughgoing restructuring of existing society, they "tolerated the *status quo* in international life while still holding out hope for a gradual evolution toward a peaceful world order" (David S. Patterson). Their supporters included wealthy businessmen, prominent lawyers and scholars, and liberal Protestant clergymen. The peace movement at this time even attracted a few adherents of the Navy League; these were drawn perhaps by that streak of American nationalism which we may detect in many contemporary peace advocates. (Uncompromising American pacifists of former generations, too, had often regarded their country as the chosen land of Liberty and peace destined, in their view, to lead the world out of the valley of fear of war.) A sprinkling of worthy and well-to-do Quakers active in some of these societies were, then, almost the sole representatives of the absolutist position on peace to be found there.

It is time now to turn back to consider the pacifist radicals whose theories had split the American peace movement in two in the late 1830's.*

(b) *The Radicals*

The men and women who had brought the New England Non-Resistance Society into existence at a peace convention held in Boston in September 1838 were not only radical pacifists; they were all radical abolitionists, too. Both causes, antislavery and pacifism, were closely associated in their thinking. However, as Aileen S. Kraditor has recently stressed, ther leader, William Lloyd Garrison, distinguished clearly between antislavery and the other reform movements like nonresistance or women's rights which he and his colleagues espoused; and membership of the various societies, while overlapping, did not by any means coincide.

In all of them women played an important role. Female participation in the Non-Resistance Society on an equal footing with male indeed shocked the more conservative peace men (including even the otherwise liberal William Ladd), who preferred to see women's function in the promotion of peace continue to be merely auxiliary to the male effort. The work of women nonresistants like the "proper" Bostonian Maria W. Chapman, the Grimké sisters from South Carolina, or the Quaker Lucretis Mott, foreshadowed the development of the

---

*As this book goes to press, I have received a copy of Valarie H. Ziegler's book, *The Advocates of Peace in Antebellum America* (Indiana University Press: Bloomington and Indianapolis, 1992). On the relations between the New York Peace Society and Federalist opposition to the War of 1812, see Harvey Strum, "The Politics of the New York Antiwar Campaign, 1812-1815", *Peace and Change* (Kent, Ohio), vol. VIII, no. 1 (Spring 1982), pp. 13-15: an item I missed in my earlier research, as I also did Ellen Gibson Wilson's study, *John Clarkson and the African Adventure,* London and Basingstoke, 1980 (Ch. 11: "Universal Peace").

twentieth-century peace movement in which women have taken a prominent part, not only in such bodies as the Women's International League for Peace and Freedom but in virtually every peace organization, whether moderate or radical.

Garrison, like his contemporry, Burritt, a self-educated man but with a less warm and gentle character than the "learned blacksmith" possessed, had been the driving force behind the establishment of the American Anti-Slavery Society in 1833. And he had already adopted Quaker views on war several years earlier, though in this period he was much more concerned with abolitionism than with pacifism. His paper, *The Liberator,* provided a forum for the radical antislavery people, and Boston, where it was published, soon become the centre of their activities. Whereas some abolitionists favoured violent means for effecting the slaves' emancipation, at any rate at first the majority opposed the employment of force to bring this about.

The intensity of Garrison's hatred of both slavery and war led him eventually to denounce the institution of government which in the United States upheld both these practices. Could a pacifist participate with a good conscience in the political process when he knew his country's administration prepared for armed conflict abroad and defended the interests of the slave master at home? Garrison now answered this question with a decisive no. All governments as at present constituted were evil and a Christian, if his religion meant anything to him, must boycott politics completely. Garrison's adoption of an anarchist position was influenced, too, by his contacts at this time with John Humphrey Noyes. Noyes who had founded a Utopian community at Oneida in upstate New York preached a doctrine of Christian perfectionism, which rejected the laws of man as well as all human government in favour of God's law as revealed through the New Testament. Thus Garrison now came to extend the meaning of Christian nonresistance to include "no-government" as well.

Members of the Non-Resistance Society formed a kind of abolitionist élite. They were drawn chiefly from activists on the left wing of the antislavery movement: some of the most dynamic among these were women like the Grimké sisters who campaigned vigorously, too, for the rights of their sex. Then there were the young mavericks from the American Peace Society who left it now to come over to Garrison's side. We have already seen how an opposition had formed within that body to its inclusive policy of granting membership to non-pacifist as well as fully pacifist advocates of peace. Not all the oppositionists shared Garrison's "no-government" views but many of them became convinced that the fight for peace was not merely against international war but against all national governments. They joined with Garrison in proclaiming: "Our country is the world, our countrymen are all mankind."

The New England nonresistants were proud of being "ultra beyond ultra." A few cranks joined their Society, and some members might be called fanatics, like the "come-outers" who broke up church services in protest against ecclesiastical support of war and slavery. Yet in most cases ultraism was combined with social respectability. Even a few Boston "Brahmins" became nonresistants, like the gentlemanly Edmund Quincy, son of a Harvard president, and at least two of America's leading writers, Ralph Waldo Emerson and Henry David Thoreau, expressed interest in their ideas, without however fully sharing them. Among the rank and file, artisans who knew how to think for themselves and sturdy minded farmers predominated.

Garrison described the Declaration of Sentiments which the Society had adopted at the outset of its activities as a "disorganizing" document, which "upturned almost every existing institution on earth." The Declaration summed up the Christian anarchist position when at the beginning it stated: "We cannot acknowledge allegiance to any human government." Members pledged themselves to refrain from voting at elections or from taking up any post in government. For the nonresistants believed participation in the political system implied responsibility for the actions of those elected. To vote, therefore, was tantamount to approval of slavery and war. "A bullet is in every ballot", they never tired repeating. They promised, too, to refuse military service; in fact, though, because of their age, very few nonresistants were ever called upon for the militia. While not objecting to payment of ordinary taxes ("tax-paying is nonresistance", one of them argued a little ingenuously), they conscientiously objected to contributing money which they knew would be used specifically for war. The whole legal system, along with punishment and prisons, they denounced as thoroughly unchristian. Whereas the American Peace Society held the question of capital punishment to be an "extraneous" matter, the Non-Resistance Society regarded it as central to its pacifism. Human life was inviolable. Legal homicide, therefore, was as reprehensible as killing in battle. Only "noninjurious physical force" might be used to restrain evildoers or lunatics.

Most nonresistants derived their anarchist views from the Bible, or at least that was where they sought authority for them. The awkward fact, which had often puzzled pacifists, that (as one of them put it) "the same God that proclaimed ... 'thou shalt not kill', bade Abraham slay Isaac" and ordered the ancient Jews to wage fierce wars against their enemies, caused no embarrassment to the nonresitants. As late as 1802 a Quaker had been disowned for denying that God in fact approved bloodshed under the old dispensation. But discarding the Old Testament the nonresistants appealed directly to the spirit of the gospels in support of their pacifism. And a few of them like Garrison himself were eventually ready to argue their case purely on ethical grounds. No book however holy, they held, might be cited in justification of slavery or war if these were shown to be morally wrong. There were nonresistants who went even further than Garrison and rejected any attempt to institutionalize the nonresistant faith. New Hampshire became a centre of this kind of "no-organizationalism", due to the efforts of Nathaniel P. Rogers who edited a radical journal in the state capital. However, Garrison, like George Fox when faced by a similar antiinstitutionalist opposition within the early Society of Friends, realized the futility of this position and he vigorously opposed the spread of Rogers's views.

The Non-Resistance Society was active for only a few years. During this period, however, it displayed plenty of vigour and energy. Quincy edited its lively journal, *The Non-Resistant*. The nonresistants also published pamphlets and held meetings — often stormy ones. Some of them engaged in what we would call today nonviolent direct action against race discrimination. Yet, despite far reaching plans at the beginning the Society's membership was confined mainly to New England, with some scattered supporters in the Midwest. An attempt was made to carry its doctrines to the British Isles, but they failed to take root there. Middle-class radicals and working-class Chartists had long been engaged in a struggle to extend political democracy: thus the nonresistants' disparagement of the ballot did not gain many adherents.

This failure to expand stemmed at bottom from the fact that Garrison and his friends had taken on too much. Their will to reform was boundless, their energy amazing. But numbers were small and material resources extremely limited. During the 1840's their interest came to be centred more and more on the abolitionist cause. As a result the Non-Resistance Society, now deprived of their active support, soon became moribund; by the end of the decade it had expired altogether.

During the 1850's the heightened struggle between proslavery and antislavery forces raised the level of political tension in the United States still further. The nonresistants, like the Quakers, faced a choice between two loyalties — peace or freedom. The dilemma in their case was more acute since their radical type of abolitionism led them to expect more rapid progress towards emancipation than the Quakers' gradualism did. Moreover, the nonresistants reacted positively to the idea of freedom which motivated the national liberation movements of the European continent. While they disagreed with the means employed by men like Garibaldi or Kossuth and felt these espoused a too narrowly conceived nationalism, still they sympathized intensely with the libertarian ideals of these movements. For the first time in the history of pacifism the nonresistants outlined — on paper — a programme of civil disobedience, of passive resistance to tyrannical government. Their ideas clearly foreshadow Gandhi's philosophy of nonviolence.

The black slaves of America, the nonresistants now argued, were in a similar position to the oppressed peoples of Europe. In so far as violent resistance was justifiable in the latter case, it was justifiable, too, in the case of the former. A consistent nonresistant should urge nonviolent resistance in both cases, while a consistent nonpacifist, if he believed the Europeans were right in opposing oppression, must support the right of American Blacks to gain their freedom by arms. The argument was logical but contained difficulties in practice that the nonresistants had not perhaps foreseen, difficulties that were eventually to make their nonresistance crumble.

In 1850 the Fugitive Slave Law enforced throughout the Union the return of escaped slaves to their masters in the South. In answer to attempts to effect this the abolitionists, appealing to a higher than man-made law, proceeded to organize a series of rescues of arrested fugitives; they were prepared to use armed force, if necessary, to carry out their plans. Many of the nonresistants participated, in some cases abandoning their belief in nonviolence altogether and in others reserving the right to themselves employ only noninjurious force. The line drawn here was delicate and to cross it was easy, especially in the rough and tumble of extricating a fugitive from the clutches of the officers of the law. "When I saw poor Jerry in the hands of the official kidnappers", a Unitarian clergyman confided to Garrison, "I could not preach nonresistance very earnestly to the crowd who were clamoring for his release."

This reaction is understandable. What is harder to comprehend is the violent utterances of some of Garrison's followers who, while still nursing a personal belief in unconditional nonviolence even after war with the South came in 1861, incited others to bloodthirsty deeds, such as old John Brown attempted before the fighting had started, and to retribution after the war was over. "Jeff Davis ought to be hanged if any man should," wrote one of these bellicose nonresistants of the Confederate ex-President. Even Garrison, who was milder than some of his fellows and never abandoned his faith that nonviolence was morally superior to the ordeal by arms, pressed for war à outrance. One of the few stalwarts of the late Non-Resistance Society to remain free from war hysteria, the communitarian, Adin Ballou, wrote bitterly: "We . . . appeal from the William Lloyd Garrison of today to the William Lloyd Garrison of former years."

The nonresistant movement never recovered from the Civil War. A few surviving members worked in the postwar years with the Universal Peace Union, which had been set up in 1866 by a near Quaker, Alfred H. Love. Although Love considered himself to be a disciple of Garrison, with whom he shared a strictly moral and unrelentingly perfectionist attitude towards the problem of war, his association admitted all pacifists to membership and not only those who subscribed to "no-government" principles. The fact, however, that Love "continued to . . . think as a Garrisonian" (Robert W. Doherty) prevented the Universal Peace Union from exercising much influence in a new age when new approaches and new insights were needed. The Union did not long survive Love's death in 1913.

In the decades preceding World War I the most significant expression of radical pacifism occurred not in the English speaking world but in Russia. Its exponent was the writer, Leo Tolstoy. When Garrison's son, Wendell, read a translation of Tolstoy's *What I Believe* (first published in Russian in 1888), he was surprised by the similarity between Tolstoy's views on peace and his father's and wrote to Tolstoy to tell him about the New England nonresistants. Tolstoy's adoption of an anarchist variety of pacifism had happened much earlier, in the late 1870's. His "conversion" then was the climax of a long process of spiritual fermentation, of growing discontent with orthodox religion and with the aristocratic society of which hitherto he had been a member. Reading the New Testament again and profoundly impressed in particular by the Sermon on the Mount, Tolstoy had come to the conclusion that Western civilization as a whole, of which Tsarist Russia already formed a part, was sick and likely to die unless renovation came quickly. A return to evangelical simplicity of life and morals was what he now urged. In his view, only the peasants had succeeded in preserving the gospel spirit in some measure: the cultured classes were hopelessly corrupted by affluence and greed. Jesus, Tolstoy now believed, had taught nonresistance to evil as part of a broader philosophy of nonviolence that contemporary civilization denied in all its activities. Man, therefore, must renounce war: the citizen must refuse military service and go to prison rather than serve in any army or navy. The passion and totalness with which Tolstoy henceforward espoused pacifism reflects perhaps the difficulty which the author of *War and Peace* experienced in renouncing patriotism and military glory: in fact he could never entirely rid himself of an interest in military strategy, and his love of country remained profound.

Tolstoy first appeared before the public as the apostle of nonresistance when he published his book, *A Confession,* in 1879. His newly found belief in nonviolence was the result both of his study of the New Testament and of independent thinking on the subject. He already knew vaguely, it is true, of the Quakers' and Mennonites' testimony against war, and he was in contact with a contemporary Russian religious thinker named A. K. Malikov who taught nonviolence and the duty of returning enmity with love. But Tolstoy's more intimate acquaintance with his pacifist predecessors came only later.

Like Chelčický and the Anabaptists Tolstoy regarded the Sermon on the Mount as embodying a Law of Love which men might disobey only at their peril. Mankind's spiritual welfare depended ultimately on adoption of this law. "Resist not evil" was at its centre: for Tolstoy this injunction transcended the Christian religion and was to be found embedded in the teachings of other religious leaders of the world, too. Official Christianity, Catholic, Protestant and Orthodox, had betrayed its mission to practice — and not merely preach — the Law of Love: other religions like Buddhism had failed, too, to follow the pacific teachings of their founders. Moreover, those in authority could not plead the duties of office in extenuation of their failure to practice nonretaliation, for the Law of Love applied to all without distinction of class or calling. Nonresistance was a personal obligation from which there was no exemption. This not only undermined the institution of property, at least in so far as property required force to defend it. Nonresistance meant the end of the state, too, as men knew it at any rate. "Government", Tolstoy wrote, "is violence; Christianity is meekness, nonresistance, love. And, therefore, government cannot be Christian, and a man who wishes to be a Christian must not serve government." The state was the arch-enemy of man: it must go if the species was not to destroy itself.

Tolstoy, like other anarchists, wished to base the organization of society on consent, on cooperation, and not on force. Since war represents the maximum application of injurious force known to man, war resistance featured prominently in Tolstoy's programme. Not only was war a negation of the Law of Love. To fight for the nation-state as presently constituted meant submission to the most powerful organ of human oppression in its most bestial form. An "instinctive" and "spontaneous" affection for the land of one's birth Tolstoy regarded as excusable. But patriotism, in his view, was an ignoble passion which should be curbed if unfortunately it could not always be totally eradicated. ("I cannot get rid of a feeling of grief when I hear that the Russians are getting beaten", he himself confessed in the course of the Russo-Japanese War of 1904-1905.) For a state was inevitably an instrument for waging war against other states. Antimilitarism, therefore, seemed to Tolstoy to be both a manifestation of Christian love and an act of defiance directed against the very seat of human evil. On many occasions he declared his support of conscientious objection and wrote in defense of individual objectors, whether these were Russian intellectuals or peasant sectaries, Balkan Nazarenes or Christian pacifists in Japan. "Universal military service," he wrote, "is the keystone of the arch holding up the edifice [of the state], and its removal would bring down the whole building." Slowly, yet inexorably, acts of individual resistance to the military machine would effect the destruction of government and its replacement by the cooperative society.

Tolstoy appears sometimes to carry nonresistance to absurd lengths. "A true Christian will always prefer to be killed by a madman, rather than to deprive him of his liberty", he once wrote, for instance. This was a bit too much even for such a consistent nonresistant as the American communitarian socialist, Adin Ballou, who wrote to Tolstoy to enquire if he really thought some measure of noninjurious physical force might not be used in restraint of the dangerously insane or of criminals without infringing the Law of Love. From their correspondence it is clear that in practice Tolstoy was prepared to relax his perfectionist ideal while still maintaining its purity in theory. While the pragmatic American found difficulty in fully comprehending the position of the Russian for whom "the great sin is the compromise in theory . . . the plan to lower the ideal of Christ in order to make it attainable," Tolstoy felt the maintenance of an impossible ideal was still an extremely valuable aid to the inevitably imperfect human being, for it enabled him to reach nearer to his ideal, even if complete attainment could never be achieved in this life. "Only this ideal of complete, infinite perfection acts on men and moves them to action. Moderate perfection has no power to influence men's souls." But in actual life Tolstoy saw it was necessary to make distinctions not always easy to justify in theory, to observe what he called a "feeling of sequence". For instance, though himself a vegetarian on principle, Tolstoy was prepared to rank human misery above that of the animal kingdom and to feel greater pity for human misfortune than for animal suffering. And, he goes on, "one feels . . . more pity for the sufferings of a horse than of a rat or a mouse, while one does not feel sorry for a mosquito."

Some of Tolstoy's followers lacked his sense of proportion. And Tolstoy himself seems to have recognized this when he once said somewhat paradoxically: "I am Tolstoy, but I am not a Tolstoyan." The excesses of the disciples must not be blamed on the master. Nor of course must the vagaries of the extremists be taken as typical of the Tolstoyans as a whole. Tolstoyism anyhow was a rather nebulous

movement: there were degrees of allegiance to Tolstoy's philosophy of life rang-
ing from a wholesale swallowing of every doctrine taught to selectivity in respect
to its tenets which might reject things that Tolstoy himself considered essential. I
think we may speak of someone as a Tolstoyan (that is, in an ideological and not
merely a literary sense) only if he accept at least the master's idea of nonviolence.
Nonresistance surely stands at the centre of Tolstoyism; a Tolstoyan in arms
would appear to be even more incongruous than a fighting bishop.

Before his death in 1910 Tolstoy had begun to gain adherents inside Russia.
Most of them were educated persons, members of the "penitent" gentry and of
the intelligentsia. But they included simple people, peasants and artisans, too.
Several indigenous rural sects already existed in Russia that professed an aversion
to violence and whose members sometimes refused induction into the army if
conscripted. The best known of these were the Dukhobors who underwent severe
persecution when in the mid-1890's their leader, who enjoyed almost limitless
authority among them, called on his followers to undertake civil disobedience
against the military authorities and ordered them to burn any firearms they had in
their possession. When the Dukhobors decided to emigrate as a group to Canada,
Tolstoy haded over the royalties from his freshly published novel *Resurrection* to
help finance their voyage across the Atlantic. The presence in Russia of groups
like the Dukhobors provided a channel through which Tolstoyan ideas could per-
colate through to the peasantry. On the whole, however, Russian Tolstoyism was
an upper-class phenomenon.

The situation was the same abroad. The doctrine made several distinguished
converts in Europe and the United States: perhaps the best known of these were
the Finnish novelist, Arne Järnefelt, and the American writer, William Dean
Howells. At the end of the nineteenth century a Hungarian disciple of German
origin, Eugen Heinrich Schmitt, attempted to make Tolstoyans out of Hungary's
agrarian socialists but without much success. In Japan the pioneer Christian
socialist and founder of the cooperative movement there, Toyohiko Kagawa, was
profoundly influenced by Tolstoy's ideas, while not fully accepting his anarchist
position. And in India Tolstoyism made a lasting impact on Gandhi, whose belief
in nonviolence and cooperative living was strengthened and broadened after reading Tolstoy's book *The Kingdom of God is Within You.* (Like Kagawa, who in fact
abandoned pacifism in World War II, Gandhi did not completely reject the idea of
the state, however.) On the European continent we find young Tolstoyans being
imprisoned from time to time for resisting military conscription. There, apart
from members of a few small pacifist sects and the occasional anarchosocialist
(who was not usually an unconditional pacifist), Tolstoyans provided the only
conscientious objectors during the decades before World War I, if we omit, that is,
those German Mennonites who opted for noncombatant service in the imperial
army and those Russian Mennonites who accepted alternative civilian service.
While many young men of military age emigrated to North America in order to
dodge the draft against which pleas of conscience remained unheard, universal
conscription in Europe was scarcely challenged as yet.

After the outbreak of the Russian Revolution in 1917, some Tolstoyans —
like the Swiss pastor, Jules Humbert-Droz, who had served a term in prison for
refusing his army call-up and would later serve for a decade as secretary of the
Third International before final disillusionment with the Stalinist régime —

quickly abandoned their Tolstoyism in favour of revolutionary violence. In the Soviet Union, while Tolstoy's name was revered and his country house preserved as a museum, his followers, after a period of comparative freedom, saw the right to conscientious objection, which Lenin had allowed, removed by his successor, Stalin. In 1929 the Tolstoyan group was suppressed.

The direct impact of Tolstoyan nonresistance turned out to be comparatively small, despite the master's expectation that it would transform the world. Part of the trouble lay in the fact that some of his disciples tried to turn the movement into a sect, which Tolstoy had never wished to do. Anyhow, it seems to be true that "anarchism — even Christian anarchism — is incapable of serving as the organizing principle of society" (William B. Edgerton). The Tolstoyans established a number of income-pooling communities and agrarian settlements in different parts of the globe. But these were mostly short-lived, except in Bulgaria where Tolstoy's writings made a deep impact. There the communitarians managed to exist for over three decades, despite the long prison terms some of them received — in peace as well as in wartime — for refusing military service and despite the increasing militarism and political brutality of the interwar years. In this harsh environment they even succeeded in publishing a number of books and periodicals that expounded Tolstoy's ideas. On the whole such sturdy individualists as most of the Tolstoyans proved to be found it hard to live together in the fashion of the Hutterites who had become accustomed to community discipline by centuries of practice. Moreover, Tolstoyan nonresistance, although essentially positive in outlook for it was centred, we have seen, on the idea of Christian love, lacked a concrete programme of dealing nonviolently with evil. It was to be left to Gandhi to attempt this with his concept of *satyagraha,* "truthforce", which included practical techniques of nonviolent resistance.

Yet in two respects at least Tolstoyism gave impetus to the expansion of pacifism in the twentieth century. In the first place Tolstoy lifted the idea of nonviolence out of its cultural matrix and showed it possessed a right of existence outside the Christian tradition. He first "desectarianized" it, we may say, and then showed its potentiality for acting as a social and intellectual force among Asian and African peoples. As he wrote: "It is not only Christians but all just people who must refuse to become soldiers." He asserted the universality of pacifism and nonviolence as a rule of ethics. Gandhi, indeed, when launching his first campaign of civil disobedience in South Africa towards the end of 1906 was already under the influence of Tolstoyan nonresistance. Secondly, Tolstoy introduced a new note into the pacifist argument when he pleaded for a radical restructuring of society as an essential prerequisite for establishing international peace and brotherhood. The New England nonresistants had sounded the same note earlier but they had quickly disappeared. In Tolstoy's own day socialists and anarchists on the political left espoused antimilitarism, but they seldom believed in nonviolence and only awaited the day when they could turn their arms against their capitalist rulers. On the other hand, on the eve of World War I the organized peace movement — not excluding the Quakers — ignored almost completely the economic and social causes of war, while the Mennonites still shut themselves off in their sectarian enclosure. Therefore, in any investigation of the antecedents of twentieth-century pacifism the Tolstoyan impulse, which combined uncompromising nonviolence with unrelenting criticism of society, cannot be neglected.

The essence of pacifism throughout the centuries has been the individual's renunciation of war. It is this that distinguishes it from the broader movement for peace, from the kind of "pacificism" which includes no such requirement from its adherents. While clearly the two are linked closely, pacifism and pacificism are by no means identical. The history of pacifism, we know, is not quite the same, either, as the history of conscientious objection to war. But war resistance of this kind must necessarily occupy a central position in pacifist history. For pacifism would lose its inner drive without at least an implicit obligation to take a personal stand against war.

SELECTED BIBLIOGRAPHY

Only books and booklets are listed here — and my list of course is highly selective, with preference given to more recent publications in the English language. For articles in periodicals and other relevant sources, I would refer the reader to the notes and bibliographies included in my various volumes on pacifist history as well as in the works of other authors mentioned below.

GENERAL HISTORY OF PACIFISM

Bainton, Roland H. *Christian Attitudes toward War and Peace: A Historical Survey and Critical Re-evaluation.* New York and Nashville, 1960.

Brock, Peter. *Pacifism in Europe to 1914.* Princeton (New Jersey), 1972.

Brock, Peter. *Pacifism in the United States: From the Colonial Era to the First World War.* Princeton, 1968.

DeBenedetti, Charles. *The Peace Reform in American History.* Bloomington (Indiana) and London, 1980.

Dignath-Düren, Walter. *Kirche-Krieg-Kriegsdienst: Die Wissenschaft zu dem aktuellen Problem in der ganzen Welt.* Hamburg, 1955.

Dombrowski, Daniel A. *Christian Pacifism.* Philadelphia, 1991.

Johnson, James Turner, *The Quest for Peace: Three Moral Traditions in Western Cultural History.* Princeton, 1987.

Ligt, Bart de. *La paix créatrice. Histoire des principes et des tactiques de l'action directe contre la guerre.* 2 vols., Paris, 1934.

Mayer, Peter, ed. *The Pacifist Conscience.* London, 1966.

Musto, Ronald G. *The Catholic Peace Tradition.* Maryknoll (New York), 1986.

Nuttall, Geoffrey F. *Christian Pacifism in History.* Berkeley (California), 1971.

Schlissel, Lillian, ed. *Conscience in America: A Documentary History of Conscientious Objection in America, 1757-1967.* New York, 1968.

Yoder, John Howard. *Nevertheless: The Varieties and Shortcomings of Religious Pacifism.* Rev. and expanded edn. Scottdale (Pennsylvania) and Waterloo (Ontario), 1992.

EARLY CHRISTIANITY AND WAR

Bauman, Clarence. *The Sermon on the Mount: The Modern Quest for Its Meaning.* Macon (Georgia), 1985.

Bienert, Walther. *Krieg, Kriegsdienst und Kriegsdienstverweigerung nach der Botschaft des Neuen Testaments.* Stuttgart, 1952.

Butturini, Emilio, ed. *La nonviolenza nel cristianesimo dei primi secoli.* Turin, 1977.

Cadoux, C. John. *The Early Christian Attitude to War: A Contribution to the History of Christian Ethics.* London, 1919.

Colombo, Arturo. *La problematica della guerra nel pensiero politico cristiano (dal I al V secolo).* Milan, 1970.

Daly, Robert J., ed. *Christians and the Military: The Early Experience.* Philadelphia, 1985.

Driver, John. *How Christians made Peace with War: Early Christian Understandings of War.* Scottdale and Kitchener (Ontario), 1988.

Ferguson, John. *The Politics of Love: The New Testament and Non-violent Revolution.* Cambridge, [1973].

Ford, J. Massyngbaerde. *My Enemy is My Guest: Jesus and Violence in Luke.* Maryknoll, 1984.

Fridrichsen, Anton. *Krig och fred i Nya Testamentet* (Uppsala Universitets Årsskrift 1940:3). Uppsala, 1940.

Harnack, Adolf. *Militia Christi: The Christian Religion and the Military in the First Three Centuries.* Transl. from the German by David McInnes Gracie. Philadelphia, 1981.

Hornus, Jean-Michel. *It is not lawful for me to fight: Early Christian Attitudes toward War, Violence, and the State.* Transl. from the French by Alan Kreider and Oliver Coburn. Scottdale and Kitchener, 1980.

Horsley, Richard A. *Jesus and the Spiral of Violence: Popular Jewish Disturbance in Roman Palestine.* San Francisco, 1987.

Klassen, William. *Love of Enemies: The Way to Peace.* Philadelphia, 1984.

Macgregor, G.H.C. *The New Testament Basis of Pacifism.* London, [1936].

McSorley, Richard. *New Testament Basis of Peacemaking.* Rev. and expanded edn. Scottdale and Kitchener, 1985.

Schottroff, Luise *et al. Essays on the Love Commandment.* Transl. from the German by Reginald H. and Ilse Fuller. Philadelphia, 1978.

Swift, Louis J. *The Early Church Fathers on War and Military Service.* Wilmington (Delaware), 1983.

Yoder, John H. *The Politics of Jesus: Vicit Agnus Noster.* Grand Rapids (Michigan), 1972.

PACIFISM IN LATE MEDIEVAL BOHEMIA

Brock, Peter. *The Political and Social Doctrines of the Unity of Czech Brethren in the Fifteenth and Early Sixteenth Centuries.* The Hague, 1957.

Wagner, Murray L. *Petr Chelcický: A Radical Separatist in Hussite Bohemia.* Scottdale and Kitchener, 1983.

THE NONRESISTANT TRADITION

Bauman, Clarence. *Gewaltlosigkeit in Täufertum: Eine Untersuchung zur theologischen Ethik des oberdeutschen Täufertums der Reformationszeit.* Leiden, 1968.

Bowman, Rufus D. *The Church of the Brethren and War 1708-1941.* Ed. Donald F. Durnbaugh. New York and London, 1971.

Brock, Peter. *Freedom from Violence: Sectarian Nonresistance from the Middle Ages to the Great War.* Toronto, 1991.

Horst, Samuel. *Mennonites in the Confederacy: A Study in Civil War Pacifism.* Scottdale, 1967.

Kot, Stanislas. *Socinianism in Poland: The Social and Political Ideas of the Polish Antitrinitarians in the Sixteenth and Seventeenth Centuries.* Transl. from the Polish by Earl Morse Wilbur. Boston, 1957.

MacMaster, Richard K. *et al.,* eds. *Conscience in Crisis: Mennonites and Other Peace Churches in America, 1739-1789, Interpretation and Documents.* Scottdale and Kitchener, 1979.

Quellen zur Geschichte der Täufer in der Schweiz. Vol. IV: *Drei Täufergespräche.* Ed. Martin Haas. Zürich, 1974. (Sections on the magistracy: "Von der Obrigkeit")

Séguy, Jean. *Les Mennonites dans la Révolution Français*. Montbéliard, 1989.

Stayer, James M. *Anabaptists and the Sword*. Rev. edn. Lawrence (Kansas), 1976.

Voolstra, Sjouke, ed. *Vreemdelingen en bijwoners: Vredesgetuigenissen uit het Nederlandse Doperdom* (Doperse Stemmen 3). Amsterdam. 1979.

Zijpp, N. van der. *De vroegere Doopsgezinden en de krijgsdienst*. Wolvega, 1930.

HISTORY OF QUAKER PACIFISM

Brock, Peter. *Pioneers of the Peaceable Kingdom*. Princeton, 1970.

Brock, Peter. *The Quaker Peace Testimony 1660 to 1914*. York (U.K.), 1990.

Bronner, Edwin, B. *William Penn's "Holy Experiment": The Founding of Pennsylvania 1681-1701*. New York, 1962.

Hewison, Hope Hay. *Hedge of Wild Almonds: South Africa, the 'Pro-Boers' and the Quaker Conscience*. London, 1989.

Hirst, Margaret E. *The Quakers in Peace and War: An Account of Their Peace Principles and Practice*. Ed. E. B. Bronner. New York and London, 1972.

Jones, T. Canby. *George Fox's Attitude toward War: A Documentary Study*. Annapolis (Maryland), 1972.

Kashatus, William C, III. *Conflict of Conviction: A Reappraisal of Quaker Involvement in the American Revolution*. Lanham (Maryland), 1990.

Marietta, Jack D. *The Reformation of American Quakerism, 1748-1783*. Philadelphia, 1984.

Mekeel, Arthur J. *The Relation of the Quakers to the American Revolution*. Washington (D.C.), 1979.

Nelson, Jacquelyn S. *Indiana Quakers confront the Civil War*. Indianapolis, 1991.

Pringle, Cyrus. *The Record of a Quaker Conscience: Cyrus Pringle's Diary*. New York, 1918.

Sharpless, Isaac. *A Quaker Experiment in Government*. 2 vols. in 1. Philadelphia, 1902.

Wellenreuther, Hermann. *Glaube und Politik in Pennsylvania 1681-1776: Die Wandlungen der Obrigkeitsdoktrin und des 'Peace Testimony' der Quäker*. Cologne and Vienna, 1972.

Wright, Edward Needles. *Conscientious Objectors in the Civil War*. Philadelphia, 1931.

NONSECTARIAN PACIFISM 1815-1914

Ballou, Adin. *Christian Non-Resistance*. Ed. Larry Gara. New York and London, 1972.

Beales, A.C.F. *The History of Peace: A Short Account of the Organized Movements for International Peace*. Ed. Charles Chatfield. New York and London, 1971.

Brock, Peter. *Freedom from War: Nonsectarian Pacifism 1814-1914*. Toronto, 1991.

Brock, Peter. *Radical Pacifists in Antebellum America*. Princeton, 1968.

Brock, Peter, ed. *The First American Peace Movement*. New York and London, 1972.

Cooper, Sandi E. *Patriotic Pacifism: Waging War on War in Europe, 1815-1914*. New York and Oxford, 1991.

Curti, Merle Eugene. *The American Peace Crusade, 1815-1860*. Durham (North Carolina), 1929.

Dymond, Jonathan. *War: An Essay.* Ed. Naomi Churgin Miller. New York and London, 1973.

Galpin, W. Freeman. *Pioneering for Peace: A Study of American Peace Efforts to 1846.* Syracuse (New York), 1933.

Holl, Karl. *Pazifismus in Deutschland.* Frankfurt am Main, 1988.

Howlett, Charles F. *The American Peace Movement: References and Resources.* Boston, 1991.

Jones, Ieuan Gwynedd. *Henry Richard: Apostle of Peace 1812-1888.* Llandysul (Dyfed), 1988.

Josephson, Harold, ed. *Biographical Dictionary of Modern Peace Leaders.* Westport (Connecticut) and London, 1985.

Liddington, Jill. *The Long Road to Greenham: Feminism and Anti-Militarism in Britain since 1820.* London, 1989.

Linden, W. H. van der. *The International Peace Movement 1815-1874.* Amsterdam, 1987.

Mabee, Carleton. *Black Freedom: The Nonviolent Abolitionists from 1830 through the Civil War.* New York, 1970.

Patterson, David S. *Toward a Warless World: The Travail of the American Peace Movement 1887-1914.* Bloomington and London, 1976.

Perry, Lewis. *Radical Abolitionism: Anarchy and the Government of God in Antislavery Thought.* Ithaca (New York), 1973.

Tolis, Peter. *Elihu Burritt: Crusader for Brotherhood.* Hamden (Connecticut), 1968.

Tolstoy, Leo (Lev). *Government is Violence: Essays on Anarchism and Pacifism.* Ed. David Stephens. London, 1990.

Tolstoy, Leo (Lev). *The Kingdom of God and Peace Essays* (The World's Classics). Transl. from the Russian by Aylmer Maude. London, 1936.

Tolstoy, Leo (Lev). *Writings on Civil Disobedience and Nonviolence.* Ed. David H. Albert. Philadelphia and Santa Cruz (California), 1987.

Villard, Fanny Garrison. *William Lloyd Garrison on Non-Resistance.* New York, 1924.

Weisbein, Nicolas. *L'évolution religieuse de Tolstoï.* Paris, 1960.